BLACK PREACHING

The Recovery of a Powerful Art

HENRY H. MITCHELL

Abingdon Press • *Nashville*

BLACK PREACHING: THE RECOVERY OF A POWERFUL ART

This book is printed on recycled acid-free paper.

Library of Congress Cataloging-in-Publication Data

Mitchell, Henry H.
  Black preaching : the recovery of a powerful art / Henry H. Mitchell.
      p.   cm.

  Includes bibliographical references.
  ISBN 0-687-03614-3 (pbk   :   alk. paper)
      1. Preaching—United States—History. 2. Afro-Americans—Religion.
  3. Afro-American preaching. I. Title.
  BV4208.U6M57   1991
  251'.008996073—dc20   90-38642
                                                                              CIP

All scripture quotations are from the Authorized or King James Version of the Bible.

98 99 00 01 02 03 04 — 10

Contents

CONTENTS

Preface

This book is a conflation of large parts of two books: *Black Preaching*, which was published in 1970, and *The Recovery of Preaching*, which was published in 1977. The former was an extension of three chapters from a masters thesis in linguistics. The latter was built on the Lyman Beecher Lectures delivered at Yale University in 1974. Both books dealt with preaching and culture, and both books enjoyed long and widespread usefulness, the former being kept in print for most of the past twenty years. Eventually, both books went out of print, which is the way of most books, for the corpus of wisdom is constantly changing.

So both books became in some ways obsolete, but no other writers arose to replace them, and some of the material in both books was timeless and needed in classes and elsewhere. The vacuum in the range of Black preaching texts seemed to demand that the timeless part of each book be combined with the more recent developments and research in the field. This book is the result, but there is still much need for more work.

Unlike the first edition of *Black Preaching*, this work has the advantage of data from twenty-five years of lectures and publications. The first edition was written at the very start of the groundswell for understanding Black culture. It was impossible to avoid a great deal of advocacy. Now some of the things for which we sought have been achieved in part. In fact, the prophesied increase in homiletical interchange between the two principal ethnic groups in the Protestant churches of America is already in rather full swing. And

7

other issues have come to the fore, such as the issue of inclusive language. Much editing was required to remove noninclusive language, but who should be more sensitive to the need, or willing to do the necessary work? So this is a radically revised edition, to say the least.

Writing this book was an unexpected pleasure, however, and very few people are ever blessed with such an opportunity to cull out and correct, after so many years. One pleasure I experienced after writing the first edition of *Black Preaching* that I hope will not be subject to change is the volume of response from mature preachers who reported the healing of their own self-esteem as practitioners of the Black tradition. All these years they had followed African American patterns with a kind of guilty conscience, or wistful wish that they could somehow measure "up" to the established standards. Now they know that their tradition is widely contributing to the standards respected by all, and they go back home to affirm themselves and their tradition, with new commitment to refine it on its own terms, by the guidance of the Holy Spirit.

One word of advice to readers of whatever culture: The preaching samples are better heard than read. This is something I should have been aware of long ago. A group of doctoral students had to teach me this lesson just this year. One day they suddenly stopped my presentation to confirm that the material being rendered was already in the book manuscript I had shared with each of them. Of course it was! So what was the problem? Well, they had all read it, but it hardly seemed the same, and it certainly hadn't seemed that this same material was that full of power. On paper, it had done very little to arouse their interest. They resolved that from then on they would read samples out loud, or imagine that they were hearing them with the volume turned up.

Acknowledgments

It happens that this revision, like the original *Black Preaching*, has been necessarily hurried. But this brief time schedule has been surprisingly pleasant. The pressure has been relieved by so many helpers that the book seems providentially expedited. So the first thanks go, in the best of Black tradition, to God.

Others to whom I am grateful for speedy input of first drafts into the word processor are Dorothy Gray and my two daughters, Elizabeth Mitchell Clement and Muriel Mitchell.

In both the original and the present editions of *Black Preaching*, I have been given able assistance in research by David D. Hurst, pastor at Pomona, California, my son in the Lord and in the gospel, for all of which I am most grateful.

My heartiest gratitude goes to Ella Pearson Mitchell, my wife of forty-six years, whose supportive companionship and technical assistance were indispensable. She read drafts and critiqued the revisions while they were being written, and "rode herd" on the bibliographical notes as they came up in the copy. The result was an unusually relaxed, even humor-laden atmosphere in the workshop. So the rigors of revision were unbelievably painless. I may never again consent to write without this member of the team at my shoulder.

With all this help, however, I must still take the blame for all of the faults and failures that are left for the reader to detect.

CHAPTER 1

Why *Black* Preaching?

Martin Luther King, Sr. ("Daddy King" to many of us younger preachers), once declared from the pulpit of the Ebenezer Baptist Church of Atlanta that there was no such thing as Black preaching or Black theology. He was rightfully seeking to remove differences and draw the racial groups closer together, but such differences cannot simply be spoken out of existence. In our conversation after the service, I quietly advised Dr. King that not all of us had such a "daddy" with his circle of pulpit giants to teach us how to be effective in the pulpit of a predominantly Black congregation. Martin, Jr., had been such a powerful preacher, not so much on the basis of his seminary training as on the basis of what he had heard all his life. My task as the first Martin Luther King, Jr., Memorial Professor of Black Church Studies at Colgate Rochester Divinity School was to try to help those who were not the sons of gifted "priests" to achieve a proficiency similar to what "Daddy" and others had unknowingly taught his son.

Understanding Culture

The key to understanding the different styles of preaching is in the word *culture:* Preaching is carried out in the idiom, imagery, style, and world view of a particular people. The most obvious aspect of cultural differences is often in the very language used in preaching, whether Spanish or Twi or Arabic. But within a given language group such as English, there may exist a host of subgroups, each with an entirely different set of experiences to bring to the meanings of the very same vocabulary. Listen to the singing of "Amazing Grace" in a Black Baptist congregation and in a White Baptist congregation, and you will see exactly what I mean. The timing is different, the body language is different, and there is a huge difference in meaning when they sing the third stanza about "dangers, toils, and snares."

The uniqueness of the Black experience in America is so important to the understanding of Black preaching that the next chapter is devoted to the history of the Black pulpit tradition. Without taking a careful look at the factors that form this tradition, one once might have been tempted to assume that Blacks preach the way they do because they do not have enough formal education to preach like the White Protestant majority. But that, of course, is out of the question today. Blacks are now being asked to teach homiletics in seminaries all over the nation. It is increasingly clear that this Black tradition has much to offer *all* cultures. Just as Black music helped to make Elvis Presley the idol of a virtual cult, Black preaching has greatly influenced the style of some of America's most popular media ministers. And now the great Riverside Church of New York City, of national fame as a center of preaching in the Fosdick era, has called as its preacher a Black named James A. Forbes, Jr. What is the basis of this growing acceptance, and what has it to do with the unique cultural roots of Black preaching?

Before looking at the history of the Black pulpit tradition, let us look at the culture of this tradition. Without Black culture, there could be no Black preaching. What is the role of culture, and how does it affect the very meaning of the gospel?

The Importance of Culture

Culture is the accumulation over time of all the wisdom and methods of a given cultural group, for the purpose of ensuring its survival. Each group has a menu of acceptable foods, a collection of proper hairstyles and attire, a way to greet people, ways to sing music and tell stories, and ways to build homes and rear children. In addition to language, and included in the language, is a way to view the world—a belief system. I am reminded of this often, when I have to work so hard to delete sexist terms from materials I edit. If the writing had been in some of the West African languages, then there would be no need to avoid gender specific pronouns, since these languages have none. In the world view there, a person is a person, regardless of gender. African slaves were thought of as ignorant when they used the same pronouns for everybody, but now we know they had a sophistication to be *desired* in a world of liberated women. Subtle and obvious cultural differences like these require different modes of preaching the one Lord and one faith and one Bible.

Africans also practiced the supposedly recently discovered holistic way of practicing medicine. The mislabeled "witch doctor" was actually well apprenticed in both homeopathic (herbal) medicine and a form of psychiatry, in addition to the mysteries of religion. A more accurate term for this expert in these three inseparable fields would be "priest-doctor." If today's Black Christians turn to church, pastor, and religion for virtually everything, it is only a habit from the centuries, going back beyond their ancestors' arrival in North America to the culture of West Africa.

There have been widespread rumors that African Americans were fully stripped of their culture by the middle passage and the breaking-in process to which slaves were subjected, but this belief is rightfully dying out. Too much evidence affirming the contrary is visible to the eye of the American Black who goes to West Africa. I once wrote a doctoral dissertation on this very subject (published as *Black Belief*, Harper & Row, 1975), but it is enough here to say that culture has an impressive tenacity. Unless one separates babies and their mothers immediately after birth, at least some of the culture will be passed on. In fact, even at birth a baby may already be conditioned to trust or distrust the environment. So if American Blacks sound remarkably like some traditional Africans in worship (African Traditional Religion), it is only natural. Slave bosses could change the length of hoes and the manner of cultivating crops, but they could not change how the slaves believed. Nor how they prayed and sang at night in their cabins, or in unlawful gatherings in brush arbors and the like.

The great strength of Black Christianity today, therefore, is not due to any great missionary activity, but to independent, clandestine meetings which adapted their African Traditional Religion (very close to that of the Old Testament) into a profoundly creative and authentically Christian faith. Black Christianity has the tremendous momentum of a faith deeply imbedded in the culture. Black Christianity refuses to die easily; decades of brutal and alienating urban existence and exposure were necessary to make even the dent in Black culture and religion that is apparent today.

This fact has an interesting application in mainline White Protestantism in America. Much of the present decline in mainline White Protestant denominations is the result of a theological-educational elitism which considers folk religion of the early American frontiers too ignorant for our times. I was once hired as a consultant, and the most significant result of my efforts was to persuade a very important body of religious professionals to put "Amazing Grace" back into their hymnal. Television preachers are not as successful as they are because people crave obscurantist ideas; people just want some warmth and spontaneity, something that speaks to their entire being, not only to their intellectual consciousness. People's "nostalgia" for this type of worship is a cultural survival from another century of American life.

The real message of this cultural consideration, then, is not the promotion of a particular culture, but the insistence that the preacher affirm and work *within* the culture of the congregation. Whatever that culture may be, it is utterly fruitless to try to communicate effectively outside it. The preacher should also remember never to fight a war with or engage in frontal attack against the surrounding culture; it is too well entrenched and one could get uselessly wasted. And besides, if the preacher were to succeed on a large scale, it would be disastrous for the hearers to see so much of their survival kit destroyed. They could very well become pathologically disoriented, requiring institutional care. Fortunately, very few people are ever successfully stripped of their culture and world view.

This insight affects churches denominationally as well. From time to time, there have been sizable departures from the ranks of United Methodism (the Holiness groups) because the denomination was losing the fire which once characterized the "shoutin' Methodists." The strength of the A.M.E.s (African Methodist Episcopals) in some parts of the South can be traced to the extent of the affirmation of their own culture in those areas, according to Frank Madison Reid III, a third generation A.M.E. preacher. I agree with his belief that the areas under the leadership of the venerable Bishop Daniel A. Payne (father of Wilberforce University) after the Civil War are the weakest areas today. It was Payne who called African shouts "fist and hoof religion," and who urged that emerging illiterates worship with hymnbooks, anthems, and organs. The areas under the leadership of

Bishop Henry McNeal Turner and men like him are far stronger today, because those leaders affirmed the African heritage in worship while upholding education and a manifestly orthodox system of belief.

A great deal of learning from other cultural backgrounds is expressed in Black sermons, to be sure, but it is always most effectively communicated by being translated into the "mother tongue"—the imagery and idiom of the Black masses. Culture is a factor that cannot be overlooked. It is primarily a medium rather than a content. No amount of concern for educational levels or correctness of belief should be allowed to lure the preacher into frontal engagement with the fundamental wisdom of the communal life of a group or race.

This is not to suggest, however, that culture is automatically sacred and untouchable, or that it is buried too deeply to be changed. Quite to the contrary, there are times when it desperately *needs* to be altered. The point is simply that what was not formed by rational discourse in the first place cannot be changed by that means. Important change has taken place as a result of preaching, but the preaching has been *within* the traditional style. The hearers have been *seeking* wisdom all along, and they welcome what is presented as an extension of the faith already accepted. This process, called acculturation, has avoided making the hearers feel that their ancestral wisdom and their own identity are under attack. *Acculturation rather than intellectual imperialism* is the preferred process.

The mainstream middle class churches of today are suffering decline, in part because their clergy have been taught to scoff at and war against the "less intellectual" belief system of the average member. Some clergy who have considered themselves martyrs to the cause of justice have actually been victims of their own estrangement from the people. If such clergy had only instructed the people from the people's own frame of reference, then the people might have gladly defended the pastor's right to follow his or her prophetic conscience. "Amazing Grace" and "O Happy Day" may have been ignored in the hymnbook, but the hymns broke out on the pop charts. They who speak the language of the revivalism that made America what it is can lead many of the most theologically conservative to concerns for justice, granted they speak in their

15

mother tongue. Indeed, the most stable base for social ministries in Christian churches may well be the religious groups with a "gut" grasp of justice as a biblical mandate.

It is interesting to me that the thousands who sacrificed so much to follow the lead of Martin Luther King, Jr., were moved and sustained by spirituals and gospel songs, which are more akin to country and western than to classical. When a message rides in on the surrounding culture, it partakes of the power and lasting quality of that culture. The results among traditional Christians and people outside the church can be astounding. In the African American community, lyrics of gospel songs turn up in the most unexpected places, and the Christian world view is expressed unashamedly by persons who never set foot inside a church. They may not be fully believing and committed followers of Christ, but they are not very far from the Kingdom. Because the Word in the Black churches is often preached and sung in familiar idiom, it is not confined within the church walls.

An illustration of this reality occurred many years ago. A Black head nurse on an obstetrics ward in Brooklyn was commenting on the various ways the women of various cultures responded to the final pains of labor. Some went so far as to curse their husbands for their part in this sacred process. But the pattern of African American mothers was to cry to God, "Have mercy!"—no matter how far they were from church membership, or how deeply involved they were in prostitution, dope, or rackets. If they were reared in a Black community, then they called on God in the climax of the crisis. The residue of religion expressed in foxholes is better than none, and it can be the foundation for later growth.

Fearing that Black culture had lost its grip in the twenty-five or more years since that interview, I asked other nurses across the nation if they thought this report was typical and accurate. Invariably they agreed and were pleased, although most had not noted it before. One eighteen-year veteran offered an amendment: "It's not just the women, and it's not just the labor. Let that *real* pain strike one of us, man *or* woman, and we'll call on God no matter what." Whatever the credibility of the sample, and whatever the possibility that other cultures are equally prone to call on God, this much is certain: Culture does affect awareness of and openness to faith.

The African American Hermeneutic

To more fully understand how significantly Black culture shapes interpretations, let us consider the implications of the term *hermeneutic*. Such a consideration may seem strange, at first, since scholars know the word as part of the name for a German school of theological thought. Today Americans are trying to get away from German domination, and Blacks are trying to shake off majority influence of any kind. In this vein, Alan Geyer, editor of *Christian Century*, wrote in 1969:

> Systematic theology, by and large, remains in a state of Teutonic captivity. The Aryan bias of Christian doctrine is perhaps the most serious intellectual obstacle to full ecumenical fellowship with the younger churches, to their own theological creativity and to Christian evangelism in Asia, Africa and Latin America . . . ; the tragedy is that because of the confinement of even non-Western theologians in Teutonic captivity very few indigenous theologies [or religious ideas and interpretations] have emerged.[1]

Black Christianity is in a condition similar to Asian, African, and Latin American Christianity. The difference is that Black Christianity has been on its own much longer. The faith once defined by the Bible and interpreted by the White man never really took hold among Blacks. The fact that Black and White were in geographical proximity was unimportant. Their worlds were far removed; segregation was king. If nothing else, Blacks were in charge of their own churches and Bible interpretation.

Thus, Black Christianity does in fact have more of its own beliefs than is generally recognized. These beliefs simply have not been committed to writing by the Black church. In fact, only in the past twenty years have we become aware that we have any ideas or serious interpretations worth preserving. Now that this self-respect has dawned, there is still the problem of a language in which to frame these ideas. In the absence of something better, we seem to have no other choice than to borrow from the existing theological vocabulary. The term "Black hermeneutic" seems to provide the handiest name for the unique thoughts and interpretations of the Bible that grow out of the Black religious experience and are expressed in Black preaching.

In other words, a good way to be sure that any theologically informed person understands the folk-patterns of interpretation occurring in Black culture is to call attention to the ways in which these patterns parallel the New Hermeneutic. This German term does not legitimate the culture, but it names a long-valid process and stimulates fresh reflection on a tradition taken for granted. Bluntly put, the Black preacher, whether in folk mode or working from a background of professional training, has been apt to trade "learned" language for indigenous vocabulary, familiar images and metaphors, and common experience. This has been thought of as making it plain, which is the same as the existential meaningfulness for which the New Hermeneutic strives.

In the cultural exchange now growing so admirably between Black and White, it needs to be said that this old way of preaching in Black is quite possibly the best example extant of the "new" approach to interpretation. Published examples of the new school are often as abstruse as earlier interpretation. The ideal of breaking out of old molds in Europe has succeeded inside academia, but it has not been sufficiently sensitive to the need to break out of the elite of society and be effective across the lines of class and culture. Black hermeneuticians are natural experts at this already, and so they have much to give others.

Here is a definition of the hermeneutic concept and task as it is explained by Ebeling: "The word of God must be left free to assert itself in an unflinchingly critical manner against distortions and fixations. But . . . theology and preaching should be free to make a translation into whatever language is required at the moment and to refuse to be satisfied with correct, archaizing repetition of 'pure doctrine.'"[2]

A thoughtful, intelligent Black layman was browsing through a copy of Ebeling he found in my office one day. Noting some passages I had underlined, he asked, "Do you believe in all these changes [in the Bible] this writer talks about? Is nothing fixed and permanent in the Christian faith?" As his pastor, I was unavoidably amused, despite the seriousness of the question. After all, the very interpretation of the Christian faith he knew and was defending was typical of Black churches only. Among the White reformers of the sixteenth century and their descendants, his faith would hardly have been thought of as "the" faith once delivered to the saints. So would it be with every other cultural group and its faith, if that faith were truly its own and expressed in terms of its culture. As John Dillenberger says, "This . . . does not mean the relativity of all truth, but it does mean that the absolute truth of God is always known to us concretely and appropriately in the forms of the world in which we live."[3]

The general lack of fruitful contact with Whites and their churches has left Blacks free to do their own thing, translating the faith into the forms of the Black world, largely unhampered by the Teutonic captivity of White theology. The fresh style and vibrancy of the best of this translation, the living, working relevance of this hermeneutic approach, are freighted with meaning for all seekers after truth, both Black and otherwise. Just as the New Hermeneutic of Ebeling and others has sought to recapture the vital messages of Luther and the Reformation for the benefit of their descendants, so must the Black hermeneutic seek to look into the message of the Black past and see what Black ancestors could be saying to Black people today.

There is very little literature on Black biblical interpretation as a discipline, and all of it is necessarily concerned primarily with the Black preaching style and its interpretative tradition. Since *Black Preaching* was first released in 1970, two books on Black hermeneutics have emerged: Joseph A. Johnson, Jr., *Proclamation Theology* (Shreveport: Fourth Episcopal District Press, 1977); and Warren A. Stewart, Sr., *Interpreting the Bible in the Black Church* (Valley Forge: Judson Press, 1984).[4] In addition to these, there is *Unexpected News* by Robert McAfee Brown, (Philadelphia: Westminster Press, 1984), which is subtitled "Reading the Bible with Third World Eyes" and contains considerable non-Western hermeneutic insight.

Interesting is the unanimity of these Black authors, which is partly due to the comparative stability and widespread agreement of Black oral tradition. There has been no significant change in two centuries in the best of Black preaching. This fact bears scrutiny (see also chap. 2), of course, since the pace of world change seems hardly to permit such changelessness, save as an anachronism out of touch with life. The religious communication of Blacks has survived, for one reason, because it was not in the mainstream of the changing world of White theology and worship. The life-style to which it spoke and speaks was and is in an eddy away from the main flow. Thus isolated, this life-style retains a number of constants which outweigh the apparent changes. No matter how physically comfortable Blacks are today, their standard of living is about as far below that of the average White as ever. This oppression may have taken on some measure of sophistication and window dressing, but the majority of the citizens of the Black ghetto are not as close to real acceptance in 1990 as they were twenty years ago, when *Black Preaching* was first written. In consequence, the fact that ghetto gospel and religious practice should have maintained character and even prospered should surprise no one. For ordinary Blacks to keep the faith at all, they have had to do so in their own relevant Black ways—inside the perimeters of their own religious experience.

The proclamation of the Black pulpit survives likewise because, in its isolation from the mainstream, it spoke and it speaks peculiarly to the needs of Blacks. Unscathed by the proud abstractions of the Western world—born in Greece and reared in northwest Europe— Blacks read or listened to scriptures and retold the story in the manner of their own African culture heritage. To a people who were not oriented to print, the gospel was preached most often from combined *memory* and narrative *improvisation*, in the common tongue, with all its freshness and relevance. A *written* version would be radically different. If, as Ebeling suggests, the gospel strives for expression, how then could the Black preached Word not be radically different from the gospel preached from a manuscript with far less spontaneity?

This illustrates two very sound principles advanced by the school of thought called the New Hermeneutic. Our Black ancestors knew and followed these rules long before the Germans spelled out the new hermeneutic. The first is that one must declare the gospel in the language and culture of the people—the vernacular. For some this involves resistance to a temptation to sound learned and "proper." To the Black ancestors this was no problem. Innocent of schooling (indeed locked out of schools!), they were so limited to their culture as to have no choice. The best of Black preachers today still know intuitively that they owe no allegiance to any cultural criteria save the idiom and images of the people. Deprived of the opportunity to be scholarly by the limitations of a hostile educational system, earlier Black pastors were forced to elaborate on a Bible story with imagination, which could make it meaningful to them and their hearers. Black folk still crowd churches in this secular age just to hear the gospel spoken in these same moving and relevant terms. There can be no wonder about why the educated Black preacher of today is not the least tempted to forgo the Black style.

The second hermeneutic principle is that the gospel must speak to a person's current needs. The Black ancestors felt no compulsion to be orthodox or accepted. They showed no inclination to follow literalistic interpretations such as those devised to justify slavery. On the contrary, they looked without vested bias for answers to Black people's needs. They took the Bible extremely seriously, but they never condoned slavery. Their spirituals attest to the fact that they seized on the Moses narrative and sang, "Tell ol' Pharaoh to let my people go!" When they sang about "stealing away," they no doubt had some notion of the prayer closet, but there is strong reason to believe that to steal away to Jesus was also to escape to freedom! Similarly, to sing "I ain't got long to stay here" is not exclusively other-worldly escape. It is the code language of the gospel of self-liberation.

Even the outstanding spiritual of accommodation, "Humble Yourself," was a message designed to keep more people from being slaughtered like Nat Turner and his followers. It meant, "Cool it—for the time being!"—a temporary capitulation to the status quo. No matter what this spiritual's tactical wisdom, its relevance and its position in the idiom cannot be questioned. It was, like all the wisest utterances of the Black ancestors, addressed to the Black condition, and committed to changing it.

This concern about need has important implications for herme-neutic, since it influences not only the topics of consideration, but also the mode of hearing the Word. There is a radical difference between listening to an essay designed to enlighten and listening to a Word desperately needed to sustain life. This latter kind of gospel registers in all sectors of consciousness, and it is remembered and used in life, not stored for reference. This Black mode of interpretation not only makes the gospel come alive on all human wavelengths, but it also has the power to motivate the hearers to practice the Word. The Black ancestors and their offspring had and have little temptation to theorize; their culture and their congrega-tions prefer useful, concrete visions to learned abstractions.

When Black preachers have departed from the standard mixture of practical mysticism and pragmatic folk renditions of the Bible story, interpreting the scripture intellectually, they have risked loss of interest and audience. It is far easier to become an effective interpreter when the congregation will accept nothing less. If the hermeneutic style Black preachers have been forced to develop happens to spread outside the Black ghetto, it may yet make a contribution undreamed of by the Black ancestors. The depersonalized and stressful condition to which Black versions of the gospel have been directed is increasingly the condition of *all* colors and cultures in this society. "Business-as-usual" in the pulpits of the American majority seems to be losing the battle to reach the crucial needs of the people who have to live in the kind of world we have fashioned for ourselves. The adoption of a "Blacker" hermeneutic style by other preachers just might help to reverse the trend. What Lerone Bennett says concerning values may also apply to preaching and Bible interpretation:

By the grace of God and the whip of history, Black people, in the main, have not completely assimilated those values that are driving Western man to social and spiritual suicide: acquisitiveness, for example, numbness of heart and machine idolatry. To the extent that these things are foreign to the Black experience, to that extent the Black man is uniquely qualified to take the lead in recasting the human values of our civilization.[5]

The question Why do we even speak of Black preaching? has many answers. After reviewing the history of Black preaching, we shall consider at length the characteristics of this tradition, which has had so much to do with the survival of an oppressed people, and which could contribute much to the effectiveness of preaching among all peoples.

Chapter 2

A History
of Black Preaching

The preaching tradition of the Black ancestors did not spring into existence suddenly. It was developed during a long and often quite disconnected series of contacts between the Christian gospel, variously interpreted, and African men and women caught up in the Black experience of slavery and oppression. To this experience and this gospel they brought their own culture and folkways. In a manner more unusual and powerful than they or we dreamed—until recent decades—they devised a Black preaching tradition. This preaching tradition consisted of the ways Blacks delivered and responded to sermons. An attempt is made here to piece together the way in which this essentially oral tradition began and evolved. The records from which I have had to work are understandably very sketchy, and it was a pleasant surprise that even as much as is presented here could be put together from the scarce reprints of books and from other documents that have become available—mostly in the past twenty-five years.

The earliest record of the "conversion" of Blacks in the colonies is that of "Anthony, Negro; Isabell, Negro; William, their child, baptized" on February 16, 1623, in Elizabeth City County in Virginia.[1] It is possible, of course, that this was a nominal rite, but concern for the Christianization of Blacks was manifest early in colonial history. In 1674, John Eliot of New England was inviting masters to send their slaves to him for religious instruction. One of the earliest records of large-scale instruction and conversion was started by Anglicans in Goose Creek, South Carolina, in 1695.

Cotton Mather started a school in Boston for the religious instruction of Blacks and Native Americans in 1717.[2] By 1723, a slave in St. Andrews Parish, close to Charleston, was reported to be reading and writing in the study of the catechism. From 1743 to 1763 there was a school in Charleston to train Blacks for missionary work among their kind. It was run by two Blacks, Harry and Andrew, who had skills in reading and doctrine.[3] Numerous other instances of training and early inclusion of Blacks in worship and even in communion have been reported.

Catholics and Puritans were among the first to evangelize American Blacks. Early efforts to make Christians of Blacks were dominated, however, by Anglican missionaries. Factions within all of these church bodies, however, opposed these efforts. The most united group in both evangelization and emancipation of Blacks from the beginning were the Quakers. However, the very rapid growth of two sects in the late eighteenth century, the Methodists and the Baptists, brought a worship style and doctrine much more suited to Black temperaments and culture. Furthermore, the Methodists and Baptists were much less prone to get stuck on technicalities related to apostolic succession, or the education of the clergy, than were the more formal church bodies. It is easy to see how it was from the ranks of the Methodists and Baptists that there rose up the first Black preachers of which we have any record.

Early Black Preaching

It is ironic that many of the first Black preachers may have preached to more Whites than Blacks (which may be why we have the record). This can be explained by several factors. One was that, in the early days of slavery, the number of Blacks who were permitted to hear Christian preaching was relatively limited. Many of the slave masters still held the humanity of Blacks under convenient suspicion. Masters were not willing to raise slaves above the level of animal property and thus concede that they were selling souls worthy of saving. Owing to the acceptance of the theory that Blacks were not human, Blacks were prohibited from attendance at worship or instruction. Even Thomas Jefferson, an enlightened architect of American democracy, raised serious objections to the human qualities of Black people, notwithstanding his own now widely known Black offspring. We know this about the third President because David Walker, a Black Methodist layman of Boston, pointedly and passionately refuted Jefferson in the widely circulated pamphlet *An Appeal*.[4] All of this affected the history of Black preaching because it worked against the establishment of large congregations of Blacks. The only place where the rare preaching gifts of some of the first Black converts could be exercised was in predominantly White (and tolerant) congregations.

Another factor was that from the very beginning of slavery, many slaveholders had latent misgivings about how unchristian the slave system was. So, when many masters finally did permit the unfortunate Blacks to hear the Word, the portions selected for them were distorted passages from Paul intended to sell slavery to the *slaves* as "the will of God" rather than the avarice of Whites. Even with this propaganda prepared by White preachers, the slaveholders feared that the slaves who became their brothers and sisters in Christ might somehow arrive at the notion that enslavement was scandalous. Some truth, however inadvertently, might be discovered.[5] At this early stage of slavery, a visible *Black* congregation was thus unthinkable.

Early in the slave experience, there were a great many masters who required seven days of work a week instead of six.[6] Little by little, the influence of new denominations prompted the giving of a day of rest, which, according to the Ten Commandments, was to be given even to animals. But the earlier denial of a day of rest was surely a factor in the lack of Black gatherings in which Black preachers could communicate the Word.

Furthermore, preaching was not the most rewarding endeavor or respected calling in early colonial times, especially in the South. Hence, to allow a Black preacher to speak to a White audience as a mere functionary under their control was one thing, but to see one loose (with more freedom) among the slaves, saying what he really thought, was quite another.

A final factor that explains why Black preachers preached to White audiences may be that the Black preachers offered not only novelty, but also real talent and power. Thus, some Whites—especially in the new denominations already short of preachers—heard Blacks gladly because they were very often the best preachers available in a given locality.

Perhaps the best known and most widely traveled Black preacher was the Reverend Harry Hoosier, better known as Black Harry, who preached from 1784 up to his death in 1810. He was the servant and companion of Bishop Asbury, and reputed by some to be the greatest orator in America.[7] He preached in both the North and the South, and he was capable of drawing large numbers of Whites. The Southern Methodist Bishop Coke records in his journal of a preaching tour of eastern Maryland, dated November 29, 1784, the following comment: "I have now had the pleasure of hearing Harry preach several times. I sometimes give notice immediately after preaching, that in a little while he will preach to the blacks; but the whites always stay to hear him."[8]

Richard Allen, father of the African Methodist Episcopal Church, did his earliest preaching to primarily White audiences. In fact, he indicates that he spent more than two years lay preaching and odd-jobbing among Whites before he turned to his Black brothers and sisters. This was after he had moved to Philadelphia, in 1786.[9]

The Reverend Lemuel Haynes, who fought in the Revolution, was licensed to preach in the Congregational Church in 1780 and was later ordained. After that he held only White pastorates in Connecticut, Vermont, and New York.[10] W. E. B. DuBois, brilliant Black scholar and social activist, suggests that the Reverend Haynes received his M.A. at Middlebury College in 1804.[11] All of the Reverend Haynes' chroniclers indicate there was a good response among those he served.[12]

DuBois and Carter G. Woodson, father of Black History Week, also list numerous other early Black preachers who preached for Whites: John Stewart, who preached also among Native Americans in his Ohio ministry; Uncle Jack, a Baptist pastor in Nottoway County, Virginia; John Chavis, a Princeton-trained Presbyterian in Virginia and North Carolina (also a schoolmaster in a private school for White aristocrats); Josiah Bishop of Portsmouth, Virginia, who ably led Whites who were willing to free him but not to call him as permanent pastor (he later served Black churches in Baltimore and New York City); Henry Evans, who started the White Methodist Church at Fayetteville, North Carolina, despite being ordered out of town; and Ralph Freeman, a Baptist of Anson County, North Carolina.

The Reverend Andrew Marshall had the distinction of being the missionary for the largely White Sunbury Baptist Association of Georgia before being called to First African Baptist Church at Savannah, where he served as pastor from 1812 to 1856. He was able to draw large congregations of Whites as well as Blacks.[13]

The first pastor of First African Baptist Church, George Leile, was converted at Kiokee, Georgia, in 1773, while still a slave. Leile began immediately to preach, both to slaves and to Whites, at Matthew Moore's Baptist church, of which he was a member. He was soon freed by his master to devote his time exclusively to his preaching along the Savannah River. He was ordained in 1775 and was instrumental in founding or at least continuing the First African Baptist Church of Savannah, which may have been meeting much earlier.[14] In 1778, the members of Leile's first Black church at Silver Bluff, Aiken, South Carolina (in the vicinity of Augusta), are thought to have migrated or escaped to Savannah to join the British, who promised them freedom. When the British finally evacuated Savannah in 1782, Leile went with them to Jamaica to protect himself from a return to slavery, and thus became the first "foreign missionary" from the United States.[15]

That Leile and Marshall were effective and well-received among Blacks seems beyond question. But around the turn of the nineteenth century, Methodists and Baptists, North and South had similar ingatherings. Charismatic Black preachers were to be found in many of the emerging Black churches. Before the day of great choirs and other attractions, these Black churches grew by leaps and bounds because they offered a warm fellowship in a cold, hostile world, and because there had already matured in the early churches a powerful Black preaching tradition.

As one ponders the rapid growth of the early Black church and the other evidences of the effective leadership of the early Black preacher, two significant questions arise: (1) What was their preaching like? and (2) Where did they get their preaching style or tradition?

The Style and Content of Early Black Preaching

In answer to the first question, there are hints of Black style recorded here and there, but it is to be expected that the chief characteristics of Black style are not likely to be treated as important in such accounts. This is certainty true of records from the early years of Black preaching. One word often used by Whites to describe Black preaching was "sonorous" or tonal. There is good reason to believe that African culture influenced all Black preachers in their use of a tonally pleasing voice, with or without intentional "moaning" or chanting. This aspect is taken for granted by Blacks, but many Whites report being impressed by the pleasing speaking tones of Black preachers as well. The White Separatist Baptists in the South devised their own preaching tone; they called it the "holy whine."[16] Decades of African American seminary students have been surprised and delighted to learn that what they know as a "whoop" had—and still has, in a few areas—parallels in some White pulpits.

One person who used the word "sonorous" to describe Black preaching was the celebrated British geologist Sir Charles Lyell, who reported on a visit to the First African Baptist Church at Savannah some time during Marshall's pastorate. Marshall was sixty-seven years old when he was first called to the church; therefore, Lyell's visit apparently occurred early in Marshall's forty-four-year pastorate. Lyell's report read thus:

The singing was followed by prayers, not read, but delivered without notes by a negro of pure African blood, a gray-headed venerable-looking man, with a fine sonorous voice, named Marshall. He . . . concluded by addressing to them a sermon, also without notes, in good style, and for the most part in good English; so much so, as to make me doubt whether a few ungrammatical phrases in the negro idiom might not have been purposely introduced for the sake of bringing the subject home to their family thoughts. . . . He compared it to an eagle teaching her newly fledged offspring to fly, by carrying it up high into the air, then dropping it, and, if she sees it falling to earth, darting with the speed of lightning to save it before it reaches the ground . . . described in animated and picturesque language, yet by no means inflated, the imagery was well calculated to keep the attention of his hearers awake. He also inculcated some good practical maxims of morality. . . . Nothing in my whole travels gave a higher idea of the capabilities of the negroes, than the actual progress which they have made, even in a part of a slave state . . . than this Baptist meeting . . . they were listening to a good sermon, scarcely, if at all, below the average standard of the compositions of White ministers.[17]

The imagery Lyell refers to was intentional. The theme of the eagle stirring her nest is typical of the African-culture use of animal figures to teach great truths. The Black imagination Marshall brought to bear on the Bible text was mature and part of a tradition doubtless centuries old. His skill was not a fresh miracle, but the result of a combination of cultures new to the English visitor but old to the preacher.

This much is certain: Marshall's synthesis of African culture and English Bible was not taught to him in any kind of formal school.

Marshall partly learned the Bible at the feet of his predecessor and uncle, the Reverend Andrew Bryan. Marshall's use of standard English must have been a combination of native skill and exposure to "standard" speech and literature. Schools open to Blacks were most unusual, even in the North. And most churches were unable to pay for a Black preacher's food, much less his training. Bishop Allen was quite typical in that he had progressed to the ownership of a shoe business so that he could be independently secure. In his fifteen years as a bishop he received only eighty dollars for all of his services. In other words, early Black preachers had to make it without formal schooling or support for their ministries, and with little time for study. Black preachers acquired the skillful use of English mentioned so prominently in early writings about them in spite of being denied education and not having time to attend school—even if there had been a school open to them.

The majority of these preachers, of whose utterances we have almost no record whatsoever, were still slaves or only recently freed. In many cases they were not even free to preach, and certainly not to study. In reflecting on the hazards of preaching as a slave, Moses Grandy of Boston tells of a brother-in-law who apparently died in North Carolina some time after the Nat Turner rebellion:

After the insurrection . . . they were forbidden to meet even for worship. Often they are flogged if they are found singing or praying at home. . . . My wife's brother Isaac was a colored preacher. A number of slaves went privately into a wood to hold meetings; when they were found out, they were flogged, and each was forced to tell who else was there. Three were shot, two of whom were killed . . . for preaching to them, Isaac was flogged and his back pickled; when it was nearly well, he was flogged again and pickled, and so on for some months; then his back was suffered to get well, and he was sold. A while before this, his wife was sold away with an infant at her breast; . . . on the way with his buyers he dropped down dead; his heart was broken.[18]

Accounts such as this leave little doubt about the sincerity and dedication of the great majority of those whose preaching was prohibited and underground.

Under such pressures and limitations it is only natural that at least a few preachers should not be as saintly and sound as this martyr and as Pastor Marshall. Miles Mark Fisher quotes Frances Trollope's description of a service in a tent in an 1829 "camp meeting" in

Indiana: "One of these, a youth of coal-black comeliness, was preaching with the most violent gesticulations, frequently springing high from the ground, and clapping his hands over his head. Could our missionary societies have heard the trash he uttered, by way of an address to the Deity, they might perhaps have doubted whether his conversion had much enlightened his mind."[19]

Trollope's evaluation may have been slanted because he was limited to English culture, and thus was unfamiliar with African culture; nevertheless, it is quite clear that not all of the first untrained Black preachers were so impressive as the first two mentioned. Undoubtedly, there were then, as there are now, some shallow, insincere manipulators. It must be said, however, that for the most part there is far more positive than negative evidence. The concern here is to record and preserve as much as possible of the *best* of the Black preaching tradition.

The Evolution of the Black Homiletic

We turn now to the questions of whence and how came the patterns and content of early Black preaching, and how the tradition has grown from there. Black preaching and Black religion were greatly influenced by the confluence of two streams of culture, one West African and the other Euro-American.

West African Traditional Religion

The primary stream was African. Indeed, the Black church was an attempt, born of a cultural and religious nostalgia, to reestablish on American soil the worship practices and extended family society of African Traditional Religion (A.T.R.). Their former humane, communal patterns were a kind of prefabricated *koinonia,* which emerged first as a form of indigenous underground Black church. As DuBois said in 1903, this first church was "not by any means Christian," but "gradually, after two centuries, the church became Christian." He added, "It is this historic fact that the Negro church of today bases itself upon the sole surviving social institution of the African Fatherland that accounts for its extraordinary growth and vitality."[20] DuBois went on to suggest that the preacher was also a cultural survival, and Woodson agreed, adding, "The Negro ministry is still the largest factor in the life of this race."[21]

It is altogether natural, then, that the Black homiletic should reflect these same African roots. The languages of Africa are manifestly tonal, and all speaking includes such linguistic features. When Marshall preached with sonority, he was carrying on a traditional African musicality. Yes, he preached in English with impressive polish and dignity, but African rhetorical style is always very dignified as well as sophisticated. Sonority is not a sign of primitivity, as is so often assumed even today.

Marshall dealt with the eagle stirring her nest, but this, too, was quite African. *Aesop's Fables* (learned in his childhood in Africa) and *The Tales of Uncle Remus* (heard from an African in slavery) are classic examples of the African custom of teaching coping skills and moral values by way of tales of animals. "The Tortoise and the Hare" taught patience and persistence. In the evolution into Christianity, the slaves simply substituted the Bible's story collection for their original repertoire of tales (as we shall see in chapter 5). Marshall's congregation responded because it was highly conditioned by familiarity with and love for this preaching style.

Black preaching is inherently dependent on call and response. African music and oral communication are characterized by considerable audience participation. The audience is deeply involved in the tale, which is presented in picturesque language and great animation. Even today, congregations of the Black masses feel cheated if no place for their response is provided. Black music is full of this antiphonal element, as well. Chapter 4 is devoted to the subject of the Black audience, for just this reason.

Generally speaking, picturesque language and animated delivery are part of a larger pattern of concreteness and liveliness. The former requires a word of further explanation. At no point did the African rhetorical tradition permit emphasis on abstractness, even though Yoruba professional philosophers can be downright mind-boggling. The Yorubas of Nigeria insist that ideas be expressed in images common people can visualize. The Old Testament is full of the same approach. Similarly, Jesus of Nazareth did all of his teaching in parables. The point is that the African insistence on images and action, tales and pictures with meaning, is no figment of a primitive imagination: It is a sophisticated principle of communication.

How, then, did all of this get baptized into the African American *Christian* preaching tradition? How did the fusion take place?

The Formation of Black Preaching Style

When a people is considered insignificant, the powers that be do not bother to chronicle their development. Thus the understanding proposed here is made of bits and pieces, as we have said. But these are validated by the strength of their coherence, and the internal witness of the Black of today, whose worship and preaching have not moved in any substantive way from their roots and beginnings.

The emergence of Black preaching dates back to 1732, according to William H. Pipes.[22] His very convincing theory is that the style of the great English revival preacher, George Whitefield, was the bridge between Black religious sentiments and the faith of the colonial White. Until the First Great Awakening (1726–1750s), White religion had been formal, cold, and unattractive. Suddenly, with the preaching of Whitefield (as well as Jonathan Edwards, the Tennents, and others), the response to preaching became very fervent and dramatic, with extreme physical manifestations.

A marvelously objective account of Whitefield was written by Benjamin Franklin, who was a Deist, not a conventional Christian and church member. Franklin said that Whitefield "might well be heard by more than thirty thousand." About Whitefield's preaching Franklin said, "His delivery . . . was so improved by frequent repetitions that every accent, every emphasis, every modulation of voice, was so perfectly well turned . . . that, without being interested in the subject, one could not help being pleased with the discourse; a pleasure of much the same kind with that received from an excellent piece of music."[23] The instant attraction of Africans in the North and South to Whitefield's preaching can readily be seen.

Vernon Loggins has said, "The emotional preaching of Whitefield brought to the Negro a religion he could understand and which could stir him to self-expression. He responded to it with enthusiasm, allowed his imagination to run riot with it, loved it with passion."[24] This interpretation of African response to Whitefield is documented by the autobiography of an ex-slave named Gustavus Vassa, who attended one of the services at Philadelphia. Vassa was by this time free, having spent many years as a seaman. He reported, "I saw this pious man exhorting the people with the greatest fervor and earnestness, and sweating as much as I ever did while in slavery. . . . I was very much struck and impressed with this; I thought it strange I had never seen divines exert themselves in this manner before, and was no longer at a loss to account for the thin congregations they preached to."[25]

One direct channel of transmission of this "emotional" preaching can be traced from Whitefield's ministry in Massachusetts all the way to Andrew C. Marshall at the First African Baptist Church at Savannah. It started with Shubal Stearns (1706–1771, converted under Whitefield on his second visit to Boston in 1745) and Daniel Marshall, Stearns' brother-in-law from Connecticut (1706–1784; also converted in 1745). Both withdrew from the Congregational Church (1851 and 1852 respectively) under conviction as Baptists. Ordained as missionaries, they worked their way from New England to Winchester, Virginia, to Sandy Creek, North Carolina, to Kiokee, Georgia, where Daniel Marshall settled in 1771. There he was responsible for strengthening a small congregation and leading in the development of many other churches. One of these churches was the Black congregation at Silver Bluff, Aiken, South Carolina, which was started by George Leile.

Sydney Ahlstrom says, "Stearns and Marshall were passionate evangelists, incredibly energetic, not a little eccentric, and rather extreme in their employment of emotional appeals. . . . They inspired many converts to do likewise."[26] It was in connection with this very revivalism that Ahlstrom uses the term "holy whine." It hardly seems coincidental that Lyell should report that the preaching of Andrew Marshall was sonorous. The emotional fire and pleasing tonality of the First Great Awakening were thus providentially used by God to affirm and employ the worship-ways of Africans in the previously frozen wastes of the original Thirteen Colonies.

It is generally accepted that the church at Silver Bluff was the first African Baptist church of America, but whether or not this is true, African Methodists apparently heard Whitefield in Philadelphia in far larger numbers than Baptists. Whitefield preached up and down the Atlantic seaboard, starting in Savannah, where he both preached and founded an orphanage. In the crowds that swarmed his often outdoor meetings, there were sure to be many Blacks. It is well known that Whitefield's style influenced thousands, in a movement that greatly democratized the pulpits and platforms of the colonies. It included the previously rejected White males without education, White women, and Africans. Furthermore, the other great revivalists were similar in style and impact. Their effectiveness was so great that by the beginning of the nineteenth century, Baptists and

Methodists outnumbered established churches in New England (Congregational) and Virginia (Episcopal).

It would be hard to overestimate the influence of George Whitefield, for it was he more than any other who gave the once isolated colonies something which bound them together enough to throw off the British yoke. It was Whitefield more than any other who not only revived a dying Protestantism but also built the bridge over which it could travel to a spiritually hungry and brutally oppressed people from Africa.

The Power of Black Preaching Through the Years

The final aspect of the history of Black preaching deals with the effectiveness and power of its communication, and how this may have increased or decreased through the years.

Perhaps the greatest evidence of the power of Black preaching is that the Black belief system of folk Christianity has kept its believers alive and coping—even when in an oppressed condition that would have crushed many. Slave narratives by the dozens recall sermon stories and pictures with *astounding accuracy*. It is clear that these sermons were so meaningful because the storytelling and picture painting arts were excellent, because the issue at hand was so relevant, and because the hearers were not mere spectators, but were real participants in the experience. There can be no doubt of the providential blessing of the Holy Spirit through this story.

One of the most relevant and vivid and creative gospel messages I have ever heard of came from a collection of slave narratives compiled in 1936. Ned Walker, the layperson whose memory served so amazingly well, had heard the sermon *seventy* years earlier (c. 1866 or 1867) and was recounting it to a W.P.A. collector of oral history in South Carolina. This is my rendering of Ned Walker's account:

Now 'bout Uncle Wash's funeral. You know Uncle Wash was the blacksmith in the fork of the road, across the railroad from Concord church. He had been a mighty powerful man. He used the hammer and the tongs on behalf of *all* the people for miles and miles around.

Uncle Wash joined the Springvale A.M.E. Church, but he kinda fell from grace, I guess. Somehow he was 'cused of stealing Marse Walter Brice's pig, and I guess he was guilty. At any rate, he was convicted and sent to the

34

penitentiary. While he was down there he contracted consumption and had to come home. His chest was all sunk in, and his ribs was full of rheumatism. He soon went to bed and died. He was buried on top of the hill, in the pines just north of Woodward.

Uncle Pompey preached the funeral. Lots of White folks was there. Marse William was there, and so was his nephew—the attorney general from Arizona. The biggest of the crowd was our folks, and Uncle Pompey really knowed how to preach a funeral. I never will forget that one.

Uncle Pompey took his text from that place in the Bible where Paul and Silas was a-layin' up in jail. He dwelt on Uncle Wash's life of hard work and bravery—how he tackled kickin' horses and mules, so's crops could be cultivated and harvested and hauled. He talked 'bout how he sharpened dull plow points, to make the corn and cotton grow, to feed the hungry and clothe the naked. He told what a good-hearted man Uncle Wash was, and then he 'llowed as how his goin' to jail didn't necessarily mean he didn't go to heaven. He declared it wasn't eternally against a church member to get put in jail. If it hadda been, Paul and Silas wouldn't 'a made it to heaven, and he *knowed* they was there. In fact, they was lot a people in heaven what had been arrested.

Then he went to talkin' 'bout a vision of Jacob's ladder. "I see Jacob's ladder. An' I see Brother Wash. He's climbin' Jacob's ladder. Look like he's half way up. I want y'all to pray with me that he enter the pearly gates, Brothers and Sisters. He's still a climbin'. I see the pearly gates. They is swingin' open. An' I see Brother Wash. He done reached the topmost round of de ladder. Let us sing with all our hearts that blessed hymn, 'There Is a Fountain Filled with Blood.'"

When they sang the second verse, 'bout the dyin' thief rejoiced to see that fountain in his day, Uncle Pompey cried out over the crowd, "I see Brother Wash as he enters in, an' that dyin' thief is there to welcome him in. Thank God! Thank God! He's made it into Paradise. His sins has been washed away, an' he has landed safe forever more."

Well Sir, I don't need to tell you that the women started to shout on the first verse, an' when they got to singin' 'bout the dyin' thief in heaven, an' they seen the 'surance of grace that was in it, they like to never quit praisin' God.[27]

It hardly needs to be said that such a message as this (perhaps without the dialect) would be powerful today. I gave a dramatic reading of this message at the end of a lecture at a great university several years ago, and to my surprise the mixed audience was suddenly a congregation, with Blacks and Whites responding in their typical ways. There were twelve trusties from a prison some twelve miles away, and they were the most responsive of all. In fact, they were determined to have me "preach" that sermon in their facility before I left the state. As members of a closed society, they—more than any others—knew the meaning of that message more than a *hundred years later*—despite the fact that Uncle Pompey's words were third hand!

The sermon titled "The Shadow of a Great Rock in a Weary Land" was preached in the late 1840s or early 1850s in Missouri. The preacher was an ex-slave named Brother Carper, and the person who remembered his sermons and published his almost verbatim reports was J. V. Watson, a White Methodist preacher. The Reverend Watson also recorded a poor White female squatter's appraisal of Carper. "Why . . . he's a posey of a preacher; he's a perfect flowing stream; he's a thunderbolt; . . . Why I've seed 'um fall under his preach'n as if they were shot, and a dozen jump and shout glory at once." Portions of the sermon and Watson's report follow:

And a man shall be as an hiding place from the wind, and a covert from the tempest; as rivers of water in a dry place, as the shadow of a great rock in a weary land.   Isaiah 32:2

Many parts ob de ancient countries (and it still am de case) was desert; wild wastes ob dreary desolation; regions ob fine blistering sands; just as it was leff when de flood went away, and which has not been suffered to cool since de fust sunshine dat succeed dat event. No grass, no flower, no tree dare be pleasant to de sight. A scene of unrelebed waste; an ocean made of powder, into which de curse ob angered heben had ground a portion ob earth. Now and den, a huge rock, like shattered shafts and fallen monuments in a neglected graveyard, and big enuf to be de tombstone ob millions, would liff its mossless sides 'bove de 'cumulating sands. No pisnous sarpint or venomous beast here await dare prey, for death here has ended his work and dwells mid silence. But de traveler here, who adventures, or necessity may have made a bold wanderer, finds foes in de elements fatal and resistless. De long heated earth here at places send up all kinds of pisnous gases from de many minerals ob its mysterious bosom; dese tings take fire, and dey dare be a temptest of fire, and woe be to de traveler dat be obertaken in dis fire of de Lord widout a shelter. . . .

But agin dis fire wind and dis tempest ob pison dat widthers wid a bref, and mummifies whole caravans and armies in dare march, dare is one breastwork, one "hiding-place," one protecting "shadow" in de dreaded desert. It am "de shadow ob a great rock in dis weary land." Often has de weary traveler seen death in de distance, persuing him on de wings ob de wind, and felt de certainty ob his fate in de darkness ob de furnace-like air around him. A drowsiness stronger 'most dan de lub ob life creeps ober him, and de jaded camel reels in de heby sand-road under him. A shout ob danger from de more resolute captain ob de caravan am sent along de ranks, prolonged by a thousand thirst-blistered tongnes, commingled in one ceaseless howl ob woe, varied by ebery tune ob distress and despair. To "de great rock," shouts de leader as 'pon his Arab hoss he heads dis "flight to de refuge." Behind dem at a great distance, but yet fearfully near for safety, is seed a dark belt bending ober de horizon, and sparkling in its waby windings like a great sarpint, air hung at a little distance from de ground, and advancing wid de swiftness ob an arrow. Before dem, in de distance, a mighty great rock spreads out its broad and all-resisting sides, lifting its narrowing pint 'bove the clouds, tipped wid de sun's fiery blaze, which had burnt 'pon it since infant creation 'woke from de cradle ob kaos at de call ob its Fader. . . .

Dat light be de light ob hope, and dat rock be de rock ob hope to de now flyin', weepin', faintin', and famishin' hundreds. De capt'in has arrived dare. [Here a suppressed cry of "Thank God," escaped many of the audience.] See, he has disappeared behind it, perhaps to explore its cavern coverts. But see, he has soon reappeared, and wid joy dancin' in his eye, he stands shoutin' and beckonin', "Onward, *onward*, ONWARD, *ONWARD*," when he reels from weariness and falls in behind de rock. ["Thank God, he's saved!"] Onward dey rush, men, women, husbands, wives, parents, and children, broders and sisters, like doves to de windows, and disappear behind dis rampart ob salvation. Some faint just as dey 'rive at de great rock, and dare friends run out and drag dem to de "hidin' place," when wakin' up in safety, like dat sister dare, dat lose her strength in de prayer-meetin', dey shout 'loud for joy. [Here many voices at once shouted "Glory."] De darkenin' sand-plain ober which dese fled for life, now lies strewed wid beast, gibben out in de struggle, and all useless burdens was trowed 'side. De waby sheet ob destruction, skimmin' the surface wid de swiftness ob shadow, now be very near, and yet, a few feeble stragglers and lubbed friends ob dis sheltered multitude are yet a great way off. Yes, a great way off. But see, mudders and broders from behind de rock are shoutin' to dem to hasten. Dey come, dey come. A few steps more and dey are sabed. But O, de pison wind is just behind dem, and its choke mist round dem! Dare one falls, and dares a scream. No, he rises again and am sabed. But one still is exposed. It be the fader ob dat little nest ob sweet-eyed children, for which he had fled to de rear to hurry on. Dey have passed forward and are safe. He am but a little distance from de rock, and not a head dares to peep to him encouragement from behind it. Already the wings ob death angel am on the haunches ob his strong dromedary. His beast falls, but 'pon de moment ob him fallin', de rider leaps out ob his saddle into dis "hiding-place from de wind." His little boy, crouched in a hole ob de rock, into which he thrusts his head, entwines his neck with his little arms and says, "Papa, you hab come, and we be all here." [Here the shouts of "Salvation," "Salvation," seemed to shake the place in which we were assembled.]

Now, de burnin' winds and de pison winds blow and beat 'pon dat rock, but dose who hab taken refuge behind it, in its overhanging precipices, are safe until de tempest am ober and gone. . . . Dat rock am Christ; dem winds be de wrath ob God rabealed against de children ob disobedience. Dem dat he sabed be dem dat hab fled to de refuge, to de hope set before dem in Christ Jesus de Lord. . . . Sinner, de wrath ob God am gathering against you for de decisive battle. I already sees in de light ob Zina's lightnings a long embankment ob dark cloud down on de sky. De day ob vengeance am at hand. Mercy, dat has pleaded long for you wid tears ob blood, will soon dry her eyes and hush her prayers in your behalf. Death and hell hang on your track wid de swiftness ob de tempest. Before you am de "hidin'-place." Fly, *fly*, I beseeches you, from de wrath to come![28]

H. Dean Trulear and Russell E. Ritchey suggest that this amazing talent of the early African American Christians had as an important source the African culture and its marvelous storytelling art. When one sees the impact of such preaching on Watson, the recorder, one wonders again if anything we do today will be remembered so well. In a sense, there is little room for improvement; the real challenge is to recover the authentic power and biblical integrity of a Black tradition that evolved when preachers had few, if any, of today's advantages. The resources of education and travel must be integrated into a gospel presentation that is still basically visual rather than abstract. And the sermon, which must have a sound theological message, must also be made to come alive in a meaningful experience for the hearer.

CHAPTER 3

Training for Black Preachers
Through the Years

One of the most intriguing questions about Black preaching is, How did the early preachers manage to learn how to preach at all, let alone so well? Fully trained Black pastors today stand in sincere awe of the sermon of an illiterate "Uncle Pompey" (see pp. 34-35), whose preaching was well recalled *seventy years* later. One has to wonder if any of what we preach in the 1990s will ever last so long or speak so relevantly to the needs of oppressed people.

The most obvious answer is that Black preachers have always served a kind of apprenticeship, sometimes formal but more often informal, under a known master of the craft of preaching. This was true of the priests of African Traditional Religion, who had to serve at least three years to learn both the worship practices and the medical treatments required. Black preachers are still formed to a great extent by those to whom they listen most attentively, often a parent or other significant person in the novice preacher's life. This is true even when the Black preacher seeks the refinements of a professional education. In class after class, I hear the habits and strengths of the ancestors, and the "preachers' kids" seem always to have a head start. Black preaching is often caught as much as taught. One of the purposes here is to strengthen the possibilities of the latter and to enhance the development of preachers not born in the parsonage.

The Denial of Education

The majority of the early African American preachers, of whose fiery utterances we have almost no record, were still slaves or recently freed. In many cases they were not even free to preach, and certainly not to study. It was illegal to teach any slave to read, and it was only because of the phenomenal memories of the descendants of West African culture that the Bible took foothold from such limited exposure. There can be no doubt, therefore, that the chief original teacher of African American pulpit oratory was the folk-religious tradition of Africa, a craft "legitimated" by George Whitefield and taught or caught thereafter with a joy and concentration that are still devoutly to be sought and emulated.

There were, of course, exceptions to the general rule that Black preachers lacked schooling. Daniel Coker, who declined election in 1816 as the first bishop of the African Methodist Episcopal Church, had the good fortune in his childhood of being attached to a young master who *insisted* on taking Coker to school with him.[1] On this foundation Coker must have built independently. He served as preacher in Baltimore at the historic Bethel A.M.E. Church, and he taught school privately. One of his pupils was the Reverend William Douglas, later rector of St. Thomas Episcopal Church in Philadelphia. As a stellar example of Black preaching it is ironic that Douglas could comment so critically of Methodist emotion and presumed ignorance when it was Methodist instruction that supplemented his training at the Black Episcopal school in Baltimore.[2]

Coker's "Dialogue Between a Virginian and an African Minister" (1810) is an illustration of the excellent command of the English language found in the recorded materials of some Black preachers of his day. Although Coker's flowery style was in vogue among the majority, it clearly reveals his grasp of both the Bible and of logic, and it shows an early and eloquent devotion to Black liberation. When Coker has the White Virginian question the Black minister's training, out of admiration for the Black minister's ability to be so articulate, the minister responds that he has had no collegiate training whatsoever, but that "God can teach me by his spirit to understand his word."[3]

This testimony that God had to be the teacher was shared by most of the ancestors of Black preaching. The fact that they spoke and worked so fruitfully without formal training is evidence that God did bypass White academic structures to give America a corps of Black preachers with deep insight and unique warmth and relevance.

Illiteracy was quite common among Black preachers, as was underlined by Bishop Daniel A. Payne's declaration that the first four bishops of the A.M.E. Church did not have a good primary school education.[4] In the first conferences of the A.M.E. Church (1816, 1818, 1819), Richard Allen, Jr., age fifteen, recorded the minutes because he was the best writing scholar and penman available.[5] What was true of the A.M.E. Church was true of virtually all of the other Black churches, and surely of the other Methodists and Baptists. Nevertheless, the very profound judgment and oral endowments of the early Black preachers were of great use. With or without the use of standard English, they accomplished the crucial task of calling together the Black churches and denominations.

The White Methodists—who for twenty years refused to ordain men like James Varick, the first bishop of the A.M.E. Zion connection—never once declared Blacks incompetent or even raised questions about their literacy skills.[6] The Zion Blacks simply refused to submit. The issue was Black power, not Black incompetence. Posterity can only guess how great some of these men must have been to achieve so much when there is so little earthly evidence of their having the advantage of education.

Self-Guided Education

After the first years of the Black church and before the golden era of the late Reconstruction period, there was what Bishop Daniel Payne referred to as the second generation of leadership. Between 1820 and 1880 or so, this generation of leaders established some trends of self-guided training which had great influence on the Black preaching tradition.

The fusion of the best of Black culture and religion with the best of the literary and religious elements of White Christianity was very natural, even from the earliest days of the Black church. The independent study and growth of the outstanding early Black preachers was bound to achieve such a fusion, because they tutored themselves. They started with their own culture, and simply added on to the Black base. Their early vision of and concern for better professional skills among Black clergy led to a succession of clergy who were increasingly better equipped. Because study related closely to books (there were no books written on Black culture), and because the White authors and teachers seemed so well-intentioned, the training accepted became more and more White-oriented. With few to espouse it, Black or African-rooted culture became

41

progressively the sign of the lack of education. As the Black community stratified, the polarities were education, higher income, and White culture on the one hand, and ignorance, low income, and Black culture on the other. Even those who felt called to lead the Black masses and who were quite competent in the Black idiom often looked on any concessions to Black culture as necessary evils.

Daniel A. Payne, who served the A.M.E. Church as bishop from 1852 to 1896, was a well-documented example of self-guided education and unfortunate surrender to White culture. In his day, Payne was the denomination's most outstanding leader and the founding president of Wilberforce University. Although he was a powerful advocate of education and a recognized scholar, he was a largely self-educated man. (His only formal training was two years at a Lutheran seminary.) In the official history of this period of the A.M.E. Church, which he wrote, he tells of his choice of study over travel (as a free servant-companion) as a means to freedom:

There he endeavored to persuade me to travel with him, and among the inducements which he plied to my mind was the following statement: Said he, "Daniel, do you know what makes the master and servant? Nothing but superior knowledge—nothing but one man knowing more than another. Now, if you will go with me, the knowledge you may acquire will be of more value to you than three hundred dollars"—the amount of the salary promised by him. Immediately I seized the idea. Instead of going to travel as servant, I went and chained my mind down to the study of science and philosophy, that I might obtain that knowledge which makes the master.[7]

Bishop Payne taught successfully for six years in his own private school, on the basis of this self-directed study, until the South Carolina legislature closed all schools for Blacks in 1835. Thereafter he had short patience with Blacks who did not share his devotion to learning. Thus, he bluntly referred to the early A.M.E. ministry in these terms: "These facts indicate the illiteracy of the itinerant ministry up to 1844."[8] In 1845, when he went to serve as pastor of the Bethel A.M.E. Church in Baltimore, he recorded: "Up to that time they were regarded by the white community as the most ignorant, most indolent and most useless body of Christians in the city."[9] His use of the word "ignorant" to describe his brethren was free and frequent, expressing a deep concern for education while conceding White culture to be normative.

His reaction to Black culture is best illustrated by a quote from his report of a visit he made to a church near Baltimore, many years later, in 1878:

After the sermon they formed a ring, and, with coats off sang, clapped their hands, and stamped their feet in a most ridiculous and heathenish way. I requested the pastor to go and stop their dancing. . . . They broke up their ring but would not sit down, and walked sullenly away. After the sermon in the afternoon, when I had another opportunity to speak privately to the leader of the band, he replied, "Sinners won't get converted unless there is a ring." Said I: "You might sing till you fell down dead and you would fail to convert a single sinner, because nothing but the Spirit of God and the word of God can convert sinners." He replied: "The Spirit of God works upon people in different ways. At camp meetings there must be a ring here, a ring there, a ring over yonder, or sinners will not get converted." . . . These "Bands" I have had to encounter in many places, and, as I have stated with regard to my early labors in Baltimore, I have been strongly censored because of my effort to change the mode of worship, or modify the extravagances indulged in by the people. . . . To the most thoughtful and intelligent I usually succeeded in making the "Band" disgusting; but by the ignorant masses, . . . it was regarded as the essence of religion. . . . Among some of the songs of these "Rings" or "Fist and Heel Worshipers" [were what I would call] "corn-field ditties." . . . Some one has even called it a "Voodoo dance."[10]

All too often the tragedy of Black people was that they slavishly followed the White man's pattern of culture and inadvertently created a stereotype of what was least admirable in Black culture. Forgetting or taking for granted the values of Black culture, which are only now beginning to be celebrated fully, many African Americans ridiculed all Black folkways and held up a model of excellence that was uniformly White. It is helpful to remember that these Blacks did not succeed completely in suppressing Black culture—even in themselves—although the chief reason for their failure was probably their rejection by the very Whites with whom they were trying to identify culturally.

W. E. B. DuBois, unquestionably the most learned scholar of his day to write on the survival of Black religious culture, made the following comment in 1924:

The downtrodden black man whose patient religious faith has kept his heart still unembittered, is fast becoming the singing voice of all America. And in his song we hear a prophecy of the dignity and worth of Negro genius.

The Negro folk-song entered the Church and became the prayer song and the sorrow song, still with its haunting melody.[11]

Here is shown an awareness of the limitations of Black culture and of its adaptations inside White America, but here also is a profound sensitivity to the depths of the Black person's soul. A sound evaluation of the worship Bishop Payne witnessed would have to follow lines parallel to this statement, rather than indulge in the use of such critical terminology. The conscious, organized efforts to preserve the best of the Black heritage are well over a hundred years late, but that heritage survived its neglect and its detractors simply because it was so relevant to the needs of Black people.

This heritage survives well because of another self-educated pastor, C. A. Tindley, who is listed by Carter G. Woodson as one of the two most influential Black preachers just after the turn of the century. He was ordained a Methodist in 1885, on Maryland's Eastern Shore. In 1902 he began over thirty years at the huge church in South Philadelphia now known as Tindley Temple. His powerful preaching drew many thousands, and is hardly reflected in his *Book of Sermons* published in 1932. [12] His poetry and impact, however, are preserved in print in the many hymns he wrote and which are so dear to Blacks and Whites today. They include "We'll Understand It Better By and By," "Beams of Heaven," "Leave It There," "Nothing Between," and "Stand by Me."

Tracing the Credentials of Black Preachers

One way to trace the way in which training improved and college-trained pastors slowly leavened the Black church (to borrow a phrase from DuBois)[13] is to survey the credentials of successive generations of leaders in Black churches. For example, the education-conscious Bishop Payne gave the details of the educational achievements of the first generations of A.M.E. bishops, right up to the day in the late Reconstruction period when so many schools had been started that the denomination could bestow the robe of bishop on graduate after graduate of its own schools. Payne summarizes it thus:

We are now prepared to see what the second generation of workers is. . . . First, in literary qualifications, they are a degree above their progenitors. Of the thirteen Bishops which we have chronicled, the first four lived and died without having attained so much as a good primary education. Bishop William Fuller Dickerson, one of nine who presided over the deliberations of the General Conference of 1880–84, was a graduate of the classical department of Lincoln University. Every one of the present eight has attained a fair English education. The majority of them have some progress in the ancient and modern languages, and some acquaintance with the mental and physical sciences.[14]

Careful perusal of the official history exposes Payne's oversight of the fact that Bishop J. M. Brown, who served from 1868 to 1896, was a prep-school graduate from Massachusetts, with private tutoring in Latin and Greek and nearly four years at Oberlin.[15] But Payne's statement is quite true on the whole, and it is exemplary in its candor as well as in its deep concern for the caliber of leadership available to the Black church.

A history of the training of the pastors of the First African Baptist Church of Savannah provides typical examples of the resourcefulness of many Black pastors who sought training. Andrew C. Marshall served this church from 1812 to 1856, having no academic training. He did serve, however, what might be called an apprenticeship under his predecessor and uncle. As Sir Charles Lyell reported, he was a brilliant success in the pulpit (see p. 28).

Marshall's successor, who served from 1857 to 1877, was William J. Campbell. The official church history describes him as follows:

Rev. Campbell was born January 1, 1812, of slave parents. Being the body servant of his master, he was blessed with the advantage of extensive travel. He was intelligent, a prodigious reader, and possessed a very retentive memory. He was a close student of men and had great executive ability.[16]

This is a good example of the emergence of leadership from the ranks of the "house niggers." One of the best ways to get an education in their day was obviously exposure to White culture. Some learning was inevitable when one was body servant of a White aristocrat. This advantage was even more evident in the next pastor of the First African Baptist Church, the Reverend George Gibbons, who served the church from 1878 to 1884. Of him the church's history says:

Rev. George Gibbons was born in Thorny Island, S.C., November 13, 1819. He was the property of Mrs. Telfair, through whose beneficence the Telfair Academy was endowed. She was very kind to him and reared him with great care and culture. He travelled extensively with the family, going once with them to Europe. He was baptized in 1844 by Rev. Andrew C. Marshall. In 1869 he was elected a deacon of the First Church and in 1870 was licensed to preach and served as an assistant to Rev. William J. Campbell. He was called to the Bethlehem Baptist Church about 1875, and by his humble, and refined and dignified bearing, won the love and esteem of his entire flock.[17]

Although it was some years after the Civil War before he was licensed to preach, Gibbons' chief education was obviously considered to be his exposure to and travel with his masters. In the absence of other credentials, these were the best available.

The first pastor of the First African Baptist Church to have a college degree was Dr. E. K. Love, who served from 1885 to 1900. A graduate of what is now Morehouse College, he represented the first wave of Black men trained in denominational schools. Dr. Love is especially significant because he also represented the emergence of a national body among Baptists, having been the first president of the National Baptists. The dearth of Black Baptist denominational historical material is largely attributable to the lack of a national body before this time. Dr. Love is also an excellent example of the kind of leadership that Black preachers gave during this period when they combined the insights of their training with the still-strong influences of their culture and identity as Blacks. The church's history says of him:

Dr. Love was also a successful social and political leader. For years, his influence was the greatest single political force in Savannah. He made and unmade mayors and alderman, greatly influencing the administration of the city. He was also a prominent figure in state and national Republican Conventions. . . . He was also a vigorous writer.[18]

Social and Political Activism of the Black Preacher

The social and political activism of the Black preacher, which was an index to competence, did not begin with Dr. Love, however. It was evident from the beginning. Richard Allen and Absalom Jones (having *no* formal training) were active in relief work in a fever epidemic that swept Philadelphia in 1793. Included in their pamphlet defending the unselfish ministries of Blacks in this catastrophe was a brief antislavery tract written by Allen.[19] He was also quite outspoken later as a bishop, particularly in his opposition to the "repatriation" of Black freemen to Africa.

Black preachers were very active in the antislavery movement.

46

The writers of four of the other five protest pamphlets that appeared with those of Allen and Jones were also Black preachers without formal education. The six pamphleteers were Bishop Allen (A. M. E.), Absalom Jones (Episcopal), Daniel Coker (A. M. E.), Nathaniel Paul (Baptist), William Hamilton (A. M. E. Zion), and Hosea Easton (Congregationalist). Another Congregationalist, the well-educated Charles B. Ray, was also a very early antislavery worker, along with many others whose names are lost to history.[20]

There were also a number of Black college-trained preachers who were social activists. Henry Highland Garnet (1815–1882) served several Presbyterian pastorates, was the president of Avery College, and served a brief term as minister to Liberia.[21] From the day he completed his studies at Oneida Institute in 1840, he was active in a group of militants. These militants broke with William Lloyd Garrison and his school of abolitionists, who depended on moral suasion to change the South. Garnet advocated what today would certainly be called Black power and Black self-determination. He was active in the formation of a political party committed to organized action to destroy slavery, and is perhaps best known for his 1843 "Address to the Slaves of the United States of America," from which the following quote is taken:

Your condition does not absolve you from your moral obligation. The diabolical injustice by which your liberties are cloven down, NEITHER GOD, NOR ANGELS, OR JUST MEN, COMMAND YOU TO SUFFER FOR A SINGLE MOMENT. THEREFORE IT IS YOUR SOLEMN AND IMPERATIVE DUTY TO USE EVERY MEANS, BOTH MORAL, INTELLECTUAL, AND PHYSICAL, THAT PROMISE SUCCESS.[22]

Education and civil rights activism continued among a small but impressive number of Black preachers. Hiram R. Revels, an A. M. E. pastor and the first African American to serve in the United States Senate, was a graduate of a seminary in Ohio and Knox College in Illinois.[23] Other A. M. E. preachers followed in this pattern, such as Richard H. Cain, an early graduate of Wilberforce University who served in the Forty-third and Forty-fifth Congresses, having served in the South Carolina Senate and helped write the state's new constitution. He was later president of Paul Quinn College and a bishop of the A. M. E. Church.[24]

Perhaps the most militant of the educated activists was Henry H. Mitchell I—my grandfather—who graduated from Lincoln University in Pennsylvania in 1876. He served as president of Black Baptists in Virginia from 1890 to 1899. He is remembered as the man who led his congregation at Farmville to place a gun in every window in the fortresslike First Baptist Church in order to protect a Black couple from a possible lynching. He also helped to found Lynchburg College and Seminary,[25] and he was active in promoting Christian educational materials.

Just as Black preachers without formal training were effective social activists and abolitionists prior to the Civil War, so were they during Reconstruction and the years following. My grandfather moved in 1901 to the Second Baptist Church of Columbus, Ohio. His predecessor was James Poindexter, a man with no formal training who is credited with writing the most powerful justification of social activism by pastors to be published by anyone in the era following the Civil War:

PULPIT AND POLITICS

Nor can a preacher more than any other citizen plead his religious work or the sacredness of that work as an exemption from duty. Going to the Bible to learn the relation of the pulpit to politics, and accepting the prophets, Christ, and the apostles, and the pulpit of their times, and their precepts and examples as the guide of the pulpit of today, I think that their conclusion will be wherever there is a sin to be rebuked, no matter by whom committed, . . . or good to be achieved by our country or mankind, there is a place for the pulpit to make itself felt and heard. The truth is, all the help the preachers and all other good and worthy citizens can give by taking hold of politics is needed in order to keep the government out of bad hands and secure the ends for which governments are formed.[26]

This distinguished pastor had been a barber in Richmond, Virginia, and in Columbus, Ohio. In both places he served Whites only. His clients in Columbus included men of all professions, especially members of the state legislature. (His shop was across from the state capitol.) His education in the theories of government came from a combination of Bible concepts and the careful retention of what he asked of his clients and what he eavesdropped beside the barber chairs. He served on the Columbus city council, on the board of education, and in many other positions.[27]

My grandpa attended school at Lincoln University with one Solomon Porter Hood. Growing up in a preacher's family in Kennett Square, Pennsylvania, Solomon and his brother, James Walker

Hood, became preachers also. Solomon graduated in the Lincoln University Class of 1873 and served with distinction as United States Consul to Liberia, Secretary to a delegation to Haiti, and head of Beaufort, North Carolina, Normal Academy (Presbyterian), among other things.[28] Solomon's brother, however, will probably be thought of as far more distinguished in social activism as well as ministry. There is no record of James' attendance at any college, even though he grew up a few miles from Lincoln University.

James Walker Hood went to North Carolina as a missionary pastor of the A. M. E. Zion denomination and built up a strong congregation at Charlotte. He so influenced the North Carolina State Constitution (of 1867) that it was referred to as "Hood's Constitution" until it was amended slightly in 1875. Included in the document was a new system of public education. In 1868 he was appointed Assistant Superintendent of Public Instruction. In this position he established public schools for people owning no land as well as for landowners, and for Blacks as well as Whites. He pioneered schools for the deaf and blind, and he would have established a state university had the Democrats not gained control and cast him out of office.[29]

Black Preachers Receive Formal Training

As we trace the beginnings of formal training among Black preachers, we must begin by noting the example of Jacob Benjamin Boddie (1872–1936), who was pastor of the Bethesda Baptist Church of New Rochelle, New York, for twenty-nine years. His theological training reveals remarkable creativity outside the established patterns.

J. B. Boddie was the fourth of nine children born to ex-slave parents in Nashville, North Carolina. As a boy he gained a sixth-grade education in the rural schools, between duties on the farm. He also attended Auburn Institute (the equivalent of high school) at Franklin, North Carolina, for three years, and taught school for a brief period. Later he ran a grocery store in Princeton, New Jersey, before moving to Philadelphia, where he worked as a hod carrier on tall-building construction jobs and as an employee of an ice plant. He was a giant of a man, standing six feet seven inches tall and weighing 260 pounds.

In his efforts to become ordained, he was discouraged by his Northern church connections and had to return to North Carolina.

49

Always aware of his limitations, he worked on a coal truck to supplement his earnings even after he was pastor at Scranton, Pennsylvania. Meanwhile, he soaked up information from everywhere. After his first wife died, he married the first Black woman to graduate from what became East Stroudsburg Teachers College. Her tutelage, his wide reading (in books and journals), and his faithful attendance at conferences at Northfield, Massachusetts, for thirty-three years were his education. At the conferences he was exposed to ideas from great preachers such as Archibald Robertson, John R. Mott, Robert Speer, George Buttrick, Harry Emerson Fosdick, and Paul Scherer. He translated whatever had potential for his audience into his own fiery Black idiom, picture-painting, and storytelling. His congregation, 75 percent of them domestic servants, loved his simplicity, clarity, and practicality. Yet he had great appeal among learned clergy and more sophisticated audiences.

J. B. Boddie, with his honorary doctorates, was never pompous, and he was never out of touch with current realities. Although he could hardly be characterized as a militant, he was deeply involved in the improvement of educational opportunities for Blacks. For economic self-determination he led his members in the founding of a rather successful real estate business, which went down only after the foreclosures of the Depression. He was also quite missionary-minded and involved in such projects as a home for the aged, which he personally subsidized. He was very active in the affairs of his denomination and was a nationally respected speaker and leader.[30]

Farther along the continuum of formal education prototypes is a preacher whose self-teaching was validated when he earned a college degree in record time. Elijah John Fisher is best known as pastor of the famous Olivet Baptist Church of Chicago, where he served from 1903 to 1915. Born in 1858 in La Grange, Georgia, he was the youngest of eight boys in a family of seventeen children. He was "hired out" by his master to serve in a Baptist parsonage while he was still a small child. Thus he received early exposure to Christian teachings and was baptized before he was six years old. His father was an unordained "floor preacher" in the Black congregation that met in the Whites' church building. Thus was his exposure intensified.

When Elijah was seventeen, his father died, leaving a request that his youngest son, Elijah, care for the farm and family still at home. Faithfully he complied, studying all he could when his chores permitted. He studied for a month under the tutelage of an ex-house-slave who could read. Tuition at this log hut was a dollar a month. Despite Elijah's good management, his next stint of study (two months with a White missionary) was interrupted by financial reverses, which forced the sale of the family farm. He then spent two years working in the coal mines of Anniston, Alabama, with nearly two more years there as a butler. Here and there along the way he learned to read. He studied grammar and arithmetic under various teachers, including some from Atlanta Baptist Seminary, later known as Morehouse College.

At age twenty-one, Elijah was called to preach. Before long he was serving as the pastor of small country churches and was teaching at country schools. While boarding a train for one of his assignments, he fell and lost a leg. After recovering, he taught in La Grange and served more country churches, before being called successively to the First Baptist Church of Anniston (1883), the First Colored Baptist Church of La Grange, and the Mount Olive Baptist Church of Atlanta (1889).

Then he entered Atlanta Baptist Seminary and asked to be placed in the senior class. He was able in preparation for seminary to augment his already substantial reading, enough to pass the required examinations. In the same two-year period he also baptized twelve hundred persons, held important offices in state-wide Baptist work, helped to improve the living conditions of his people, edited a newspaper for Blacks, and personally invested in and helped to promote various economic enterprises. He was an outspoken defender of civil rights and was not afraid to demand equality for Blacks under the Constitution.

Elijah Fisher's only year of formal training came after many years of success as a minister and teacher. His degree no doubt required the study of Hebrew and Greek. Thereafter, he spent many hours in his own fine library, and was known, among other things, as an intellectual giant in the Black church.

After seminary Dr. Fisher served two years at the Spruce Street Baptist Church of Nashville, Tennessee, after which he went to Chicago. There he repeated his successes in building churches and resolving debts. During his twelve years in Chicago, he built a church reputed to be the largest Protestant congregation in the world. He launched the church in impressive programs for youth and he stimulated the youth to seek college preparation. He fostered performances by Black artists and constantly supported Black economic activities, both through the church and through personal investment. These activities included land and mining ventures, a coal and gas business, a print shop, and a drugstore. He provided free meals for the needy and pursued other humanitarian enterprises.

Elijah John Fisher had a clear-eyed devotion to the welfare of his people. He, along with Archibald Carey, Sr. (later an A.M.E. bishop), was very active in the Republican party, and he used his influence to good advantage. He was unsparingly outspoken against quietistic pastors who left progress to God. He publicly criticized Booker T. Washington for his silence on mob violence and lynching. His busy and fruitful career ended when he was fifty-seven, but his record as a student, pastor, and prophet will seldom be equaled.[31]

The Emergence of African American Seminaries

One might assume that the next "level" of training for Black preachers would have been what is presently thought of as the standard process: four years of college and three years of seminary. It was not so. A preacher with a seminary degree from the South was often required in the North to study an extra year, to "standardize" previous preparation, in order to do further graduate work. As late as the 1950s, Oberlin Graduate School of Theology still required that extra year. Only an individual of the brashness and brilliance of a Vernon Johns could bypass regulations.[32]

Gradually there emerged a group of African American seminaries with full accreditation by the Association of Theological Schools. Gammon Theological Seminary (United Methodist, founded in 1869 as Clark College), located in Atlanta, was joined in 1958 by three other schools to form the *Interdenominational Theological Center*. (Originally, all four schools had been college religion departments, enroute to becoming seminaries.) These were Morehouse School of Religion, founded in 1867 as Atlanta Baptist Seminary; Turner Theological Seminary, founded in 1885 by the A.M.E. Church as Morris Brown College; and Phillips School of Theology, founded in 1882 by the C.M.E. Church as Lane College. Johnson C. Smith Seminary, founded in 1867 by the Northern Presbyterians, was moved to Atlanta from the college of the same name in Charlotte, North Carolina, and was added in 1969. In 1970, the Church of God in Christ founded a new seminary and added it to I.T.C. It was

52

named Charles H. Mason Theological Seminary, after the founder of the denomination.

The second largest African American Seminary is the *Howard University School of Divinity,* whose college was founded in 1867. The seminary began to emerge as early as 1871. It has historic ties with what is now known as the United Church of Christ.

The last of the three fully accredited Black seminaries is *The School of Theology of Virginia Union University,* founded as a college in 1865 by the Baptists. Its seminary was added in 1941.

African American Seminaries in stages of progress nearing full accreditation are *Payne Theological Seminary* at Wilberforce University (A.M.E., 1856); *Hood Theological Seminary* at Livingstone College (A.M.E. Zion, 1879); and *Shaw Divinity School,* which grew out of Shaw University (Baptist, 1865).

Total registration in these six schools in the 1990s is more than 700. In addition, there are more than 1,000 African American students in predominantly White seminaries, one of which has an African American president (Chicago Theological Seminary).

Black Preaching Comes into Its Own

There began in the "sixties" a serious movement toward the understanding and appreciation of Black culture, including religion. Whole curricula are now available for training religious professionals to relate to the African American masses in their own folkways and culture. It is understood that African American folkways are not lower than other folkways; they are merely different. In such areas as preaching, the best of the African American tradition is good not only for Black churches but also for all churches and cultures. As a result, cultural disparities among Blacks are less important, and the old problem of placing trained pastors in free churches (denominations without bishops) has almost disappeared.

Many of the largest and fastest growing churches in Black America are served by highly sophisticated clergy with training of great prestige. At last, Black preaching has come into its own, with the understanding that it comprises a wide variety of styles. This is quite clear when one ponders the fact that Riverside Church in uptown Manhattan has called James Forbes, an African American of Pentecostal background, as pastor. We have arrived at a place where professionally educated Blacks succeed in feeding not only other professionals but also *all* of the flock, whatever their status and training. The growth of their churches bodes well for the future of the faith.

Earned doctorates—both research and professional—are fairly common among Black pastors today. In fact, the number reflects the longstanding romance of Blacks with education. The minute it was possible after the Civil War, the ex-slaves launched a struggle for learning which is still alive and well, even though the public school systems have discouraged many. The evidence of the pastoral ideals of schooling is seen when a Martin Luther King, Jr., with a Ph.D. from Boston University, chooses a church rather than a professorship. The evidence is seen in the life of C.M.E. Bishop Joseph A. Johnson, whose heart was in the church. He received an S.T.D. in theology from Iliff School of Theology in Denver, and a Ph.D. in New Testament from Vanderbilt University in Nashville. Likewise, O. T. Jones, Jr., pastor of Holy Temple Church of God in Christ (Philadelphia) and a prominent bishop of that fast-growing denomination, received an S.T.D. from Temple University. Here and there across the nation are pastors who quietly hold the terminal degree and preach the gospel to ordinary people with both deep insight and great power.

There are also many bivocational Black pastors who, in addition to being pastors, are lawyers, teachers, social workers, dentists, or other trained professionals. Many pastors are important players in government, such as Pastor William H. Gray III of Bright Hope Baptist Church in Philadelphia, who is a member of Congress.

The Black pulpit tradition has not changed greatly since pastors were elected to Congress during the Reconstruction, and there are many who would say that their pastors' wide-ranging involvements have only enriched the Word communicated. The rank and file of trained clergy in the Black church, however, are like the rank and file of other ethnic groups. Many of the very finest preachers in the pulpits of America have only the M. Div. or the B.D. I studied under premier preaching teachers, such as Harry Emerson Fosdick and George Buttrick, whom I recall as having no earned doctorates but awesome honoraries. The same is true of the man I regard as the greatest preacher of my lifetime, Gardner C. Taylor, an African American, pastor of the Concord Baptist Church of Christ in Brooklyn.

The growth and development of preaching in the African American pulpit and in the churches and classrooms of America will proceed best when it is clear that the genius of a Gardner C. Taylor is only in part owing to an education. An education merely adds to the irreplaceable factors of sonship to a great preacher-father and native personal gifts chargeable only to God. No number of books such as this, or the best of theological training, will ever contribute more than an essential focus and refinement to "finish off" the marvelous heritage and personal gifts of whomsoever God has called. It is my hope that the sketches of prototypes in this chapter will be useful to all types and conditions of people, particularly to those who already have the call and who need a mirror in which to see more clearly their heritage and gifts.

Chapter 4

The Black Approach
to the Bible

Any understanding of Black preaching must include a sensitivity to the multifaceted Black-culture approach to the Bible, because Black preaching has been centered in the Bible throughout its history. Black congregations do not ask what is a preacher's personal opinion. They want to know what *God* has said through the preacher's encounter with the Word.

There are exceptions, of course, such as a few gifted preachers who manage to achieve great impact without the discipline of a biblical text. Occasionally a Black congregation accepts a convincing topical preacher who does not cite extensive biblical authority. But the vast majority of Black preaching, and probably the best of Black preaching, is based on biblical authority and biblical insights. Such preaching is likely to issue forth as the exposition of a biblical passage. No matter how creative or inventive Black preachers may be, in the culture of the Black church they must appear to exercise their freedom within the limits of that vast and profound reservoir of truth called the Bible.

The Bible as Oral Tradition

The tremendous authority of the Bible was originally the result, in large measure, of African traditional survivals. The slaves adopted and adapted the holy wisdom of their conquerors because African culture assumed it *wise* to learn as much as possible about the gods who gave the enemy victory, in spite of their own gods. Once language changes had robbed them of their own proverbs and other holy wisdom, the process of adaptation was accelerated. This process, however, did not stop where it might be expected. Exposed in depth to the Old Testament, the slaves found it amazingly similar to their traditional faith. There were many parallels, such as the Tower of Babel, a female source of evil, and a deception story quite similar to Jacob's story. The word *tribe* in the Old Testament means extended family society, just as it does in West Africa. They knew God to be just, provident, omnipotent, omniscient. Their praise names for God consisted of these very theological adjectives. When they got to the New Testament, Galatians 6:7-9 bespoke a law of identical harvest long familiar in African proverbs. They understood well the tale of the Exodus and devised a spiritual song to celebrate it ("Go Down, Moses"). They needed only the rest of the Bible, Jesus, and hell to be thoroughly and speedily Christian. And the love they quickly developed for the Jesus who was "'buked and scorned" like them was monumental.[1] Witness the tender Christmas spiritual, "Sweet Lil' Jesus Boy."

The Bible filled the void once occupied by an awesomely authoritative oral tradition. This is not quite the same as saying that these African Americans were "bibliolaters," or idolaters of the printed page. Nor are they to be confused with "inerrantists," those oblivious of what scientific insights have to say to rigid literalism in biblical interpretation. Black dependence on scripture is not in the mode of either "Modernists" or "Fundamentalists." The difference is subtle: A Black preacher is more likely to say, "Didn't he say it!" as one quoting a beloved parent. The preacher would not be pompous about what "the word of God declares!" or "my Bible says." The implications may be similar in the abstract, but in the concrete and experiential, the African American is quoting an ancestor, in the manner of the *oral tradition*. It is typical of the way the Old Testament was handed down, and the ways African Traditional Religion is passed on. Then and now there is great respect for the Word, yet a deep and dynamic awareness of God as the author of truth and the Lord of *all* reality. Religious truth is neither science nor history per se; it is the Word, and there is no conflict with other truth.

This rather personal aspect of oral tradition bears further explanation. It is like the Hebrew oral tradition, which spoke of the deity as "God of Abraham, Isaac, and Jacob." God was best understood by means of the talk and walk of the ancestors: the lived life and spoken words of parents, grandparents, and great-grandparents. The ancestors had great authority as persons, and their devotion to God's Word imparted to it all of their influence as persons to add to its own authority.

In the African American community, the Bible is often quoted with the opening, "My mother (or father or grandfather or grandmother) always told me . . . ." So it is quite normal that a great preacher like Howard Thurman would often speak of his grandmother as the catalyst of some of his most profound insights. It was she who bestirred the root ideas of his classic *Jesus and the Disinherited,*[2] because it was she who cared for him and for whom he read. The parts of the Bible dear to her were his Bible as well.

The legendary president of Morehouse College, Benjamin E. Mays, with his clear commitment to Western learning, unashamedly ascribed to his mother's prayer habits (and to his own) his victory in the struggle to break away from the farm and to get an education.[3] The versatile artist and current professor Maya Angelou illustrated often the power of the oral religious tradition in African American culture in her autobiographical *I Know Why the Caged Bird Sings.*[4] It was her grandmother, far more than preachers or teachers, who gave her the foundations for her now widely sought religious expressions.

It is on such a base as this that the Black preacher of today still uses scripture for the interpretation of God's way and will for people. The very literal, impersonal use of the scriptures would be foreign to this preacher's mind and spirit. The idea of an "I-believe-more-completely-than-thou" contest would be unthinkable. Trust in the perfectness of one's abstract statement of faith would be a form of works-salvation. The Black Bible is a *living* epistle, and the elaborations never take the form of coldly abstract formulations.

The Black preacher is more apt to think of the BIble as an inexhaustible source of good preaching material than as an inert doctrinal and ethical authority. It is full of insights—warm and wise and relevant to the everyday problems of Black people. It provides the basis for unlimited creativity in the telling of rich and interesting stories, and these narrations command rapt attention while the eternal truth is brought to bear on the struggle to survive and to find a measure of dignity and freedom. The Bible's authority undergirds remembrance and provides permanent reference points for discernment and to help illuminate whatever the Holy Spirit gives the preacher to say.

The best of Black preachers do not merely use the Bible; they let the Bible use them. Their intuitively flexible approach to the Bible leads them to ask, "In this passage of scripture, what is the Lord trying to tell me today?" Or, "What answer for today's need can be found somewhere in this New Testament?" (Off the record, the preacher may be probing for what Grandma would reach into the Bible for to quote for the purpose.) The preacher then asks, "How may I see it and tell it in the images and idiom of my people, so that it will be real and life-changing?" The Black preacher is not in favor of pat, easy, legalistic, or literalistic answers. The unspoken but intuitive goal is an *experience* of the Word, which plants the Word deep in human consciousness.

The Black preacher avoids dead, irrelevant formulations, no matter how normative they may have been in the past. When caught using such crutches, the Black preacher is probably desperate for material and grabbing for straws. The wellsprings of vital faith have been clogged, often by an acquired dependence on sources outside the flow of the belief system of the vibrant ancestors.

Gospel, Not Science

At the best of the tradition, the Black preacher is not as concerned with historical or scientific truth as with what might be called affirmations of faith. There is no intention of making the Bible a science textbook. For one thing, during a stirring sermon, there is little or no interest in science. Rather, the interest is in the Bible as a reliable index to God's word and will. In this broader concern, science finds its proper role or perspective as just one way of talking about God's larger reality.

This stance seems to be congruent with that of the Gospel writers at the time they wrote. Their intent was to record what had already been widely preached in the churches. It would probably never have crossed the mind of someone such as Luke that the *kerygma* was anything but a resource for preaching. Luke would certainly never have thought of it as a resource for literalistic resistance to science, a book that could claim to know as much about natural or physical phenomena as about God's will. The Black devotion to the Bible is not anti-intellectual; it simply and wisely avoids intellectual*isms*.

One stream in Western thought takes the Bible lightly because it reads it too literally, and therefore views it with distrust. Another stream takes it too literally, right off the surface, and squelches the life of the Spirit as well as the dynamic relevance of the Word.

Within their unshakable attachment to the Bible, Black preachers have some interesting and creative ways of avoiding intellectual dead ends. The focus is not on scientific-historical truth, but truth for the life of the spirit. This excerpt from a sermon I preached to a congregation that included students known to have intellectual problems with the big fish in the story of Jonah illustrates this focus:

You know, the book of Jonah is one of the most important books of the Old Testament, but not because of the whale. The sea creature is not essential to the purpose of the story. And Nineveh never was that big: sixty miles around, three days' journey. The book of Jonah is about something much more important: race prejudice. It's a parable or a coded message about race hatred. It's like the parable of the good Samaritan. It leads the hearer indirectly up to something you couldn't say directly.

Jonah is also the funniest Bible story I know. If you read the third verse of the fourth chapter, you see Jonah sitting there in the city he had saved, mad and heartbroken and fussing at God. He didn't even want to live any more. You know why? 'Cause God had made him preach an eight-word sermon, and he had saved over a million "White folks." Now get this: He was heartless mad because now these Gentiles he hated weren't going to hell. A dude has to be awful prejudiced and bitter to save that many people and then be suicidal sorry he might see them in heaven. Now, just between you and me, the writer was talking to the whole bitter, prejudiced Jewish church of his time. It's no wonder why he had to put it in a parable!

This interpretation was given and received with reverent humor, and the response of the high school and college youth present was one of deep relief and gratitude. They were off the hook to answer any questions raised about a three-day sojourn in the belly of a big fish, with no oxygen. In subsequent discussions, they enlarged on the role of the Bible as a book about life in Christ, rather than a textbook of scientific detail. They also got tickled often about Jonah, and their loyalty to the Bible was strengthened.

Creative Use of Scholarship

The best of Black preaching today uses scholarly insights for more than solving imagined tensions between science and religion, or faith and reason. Black preachers often use the best of biblical scholarship to add living details that would not otherwise be evident to the laity. These fresh insights are used to enhance the gripping realism of a message. It must never be assumed that such scholarly insights are sought and used only by those who are formally trained. Some of the most creative and imaginative uses of details from archaeological and anthropological research are made by preachers with no degrees but with great gifts from God and such great dedication to the task of preaching that they spend most of their time reading, meditating, and preparing to preach.

One of the best illustrations of the creative use of details came to me secondhand from a Tennessee pastor, who had heard a Mississippi pastor preach about handicapped heroes. The text was Judges 20:16:

Among all this people there were seven hundred chosen men lefthanded; every one could sling stones at an hair breadth, and not miss.

The use of scholarly findings related to the history and significance of left-handedness in Jewish culture.

The Mississippi pastor discovered that the Hebrew word for *left-handed* meant literally "bound in the right hand." He probably assumed from the fact that there is no other word for left-handedness that one would *never* use his left if he could possibly still use his right. In Hebrew culture the right hand was, after all, the hand of strength, blessing, and unique capacity, as well as the hand of dignity and honor. The place at the right hand of God was the ultimate position. Starting from this, the rest was easy for the inspired creativity of the Black pastor.

Umhampered by any awareness that at least some scholars think Benjamites had a special tradition of left-handedness, and deducing that seven hundred men could hardly have been *born* bound in the right hand, he was on good ground to assume that they must have been wounded in previous battles or wars. They were the *disabled veterans* of their day. But obviously, they did not accept honorable discharges and disability checks. Instead, they went into a new kind of training camp and practiced until they could use their left hand to sling a stone at a target the width of a hair and not miss.

The fact that the Benjamites turned back forces ten times their size on two days in a row seems to stem largely from their sharpshooting.

Their refusal to use their handicaps for an excuse was responsible for one tribe nearly defeating the other eleven. The preacher made it plain, in a moving way, that the question, under God, is not, How much are you handicapped? but, How much do you want to work at overcoming and compensating for it?

In his unforgettable climax he pictured men with mangled right hands and arms, marching with high spirits to the war front, with this word to all who chanced to meet them: "If you see my mom or my dad, tell them I won't be home for a while. The war ain't over!" So saying he clinched the point that so long as the war is on, so long as there is need and injustice, no Black man can plead his handicap and do nothing. With dedication and concentration one can make as crucial a contribution to the struggle as did these disfigured and handicapped heroes. Preaching could hardly be more relevant or more inspiring.

The Black church's capacity to receive, appreciate, and use scholarly understanding is often overlooked. The issue is not so much how scholarly or intellectual the message, as how well the idea is translated. Fred Sampson, pastor of Detroit's Tabernacle Baptist Church, was very warmly received by hundreds of women from all over America at an annual session of the National Baptist Convention, U.S.A., Inc., when he included the following in a training lecture-sermon:

I do not have time to go into it in depth, but there are certain words you ought to have in your vocabulary . . . in your talking vocabulary. The word "Canon" c-a-n-o-n, "apocryphal" . . . "versions," "translations." As you know, in the first century people lived in what is known as the oral tradition. They did not have a *written* record as you and I have. You have the Old Testament canon and the New Testament canon. They were not blessed to go to a table and get the Bible as we have it. . . . This is why Ezra read openly, publicly from the Holy Bible, the . . . fragments as we call them today. There are blessings that we have and we are unaware of our blessings. We take too lightly things that God has given us, and others have died for what we just throw around.

"Canon" comes from the Greek word meaning "straight rod." The New Testament canon. There were many other books to be tested. Canon . . . can be figuratively interpreted as a straight rule, or, as you find it in Galatians, a rule of life . . . to measure, to document, to authenticate. And so these books by scholars were gathered together and studied, and they had to meet a straight rod—to classify them, to place them . . . in a . . . system. And so these are the books that have been set aside from the others. They are the authoritative books; they are the inspired word of God.

Now the Apocrypha makes up a set of books that has been accepted, but they are questionable in their authority. If you look in a *big* . . . Bible, you'll find between the Old Testament and the New Testament the . . . rest of Ezra, the rest of Daniel, etc., on questionable authority [mentions the translations, versions, and languages]. . . .
Now don't worry about whether this Bible is true or not. Canonized. The word of God. God breathed. Men inspired. God through eternity dictating to them . . . truly the Word of God.

On paper this may not seem very much like Black culture, but the delivery made it much more so. And the point is that the delivery-translation made it quite acceptable and appreciated, even enjoyed.

Imaginative Elaboration

The imaginative use of the helpful insights of scholars is only a small part of a much broader use of imagination to put flesh on the often skeletal narratives of the Bible—to breathe life into both the story and the truth it teaches. In addition to the scholar's details, there is a great need for more vivid but not less valid details, often not given in the Bible or anywhere else. These details help the hearer to be caught up in the experience being narrated and, as a result, to understand better and to be moved to change. Black preaching, at its best, is rich in the imaginative supply of these details and in their dramatic use in telling the Gospel stories.
One aspect of this broader imaginative tradition is that of the simple elaboration of a single word or phrase. The following excerpts from taped sermons are random examples:

"But whom say ye that I am?" Jesus said, "Now look, I want to get all this straight now. . . . You don't insult *any*body to call him John the Baptist, because I gave him the highest compliment that any man has ever received from me. Anybody would like to be Jeremiah or Elias. . . . But you see what you are saying is that I am not *any*body."   —Fred Sampson

"Teach us to pray." Jesus' disciples were good Jews. Every good male Jew was the household priest and head of the church in his house. And surely every Jew knows how to pray. The Psalms are *full* of prayer, and everywhere one looks in the religion of the Jews . . . one sees prayer. But strangely, as you read in Luke the eleventh chapter . . . you hear the disciples saying, "Lord, John taught *his* disciples to pray. And prayer is the heart of *every* faith. And we have heard *you* pray. And we've been close enough at times to know that you don't quite *pray* like we pray. And since we want to follow what *you* have to say—since you are praying differently and teaching differently—we want you to teach *us* to pray."   —Henry H. Mitchell

Paul—a little, deformed wanderer with the label of Tarsus on his baggage.   —Gardner C. Taylor

The man on that ship that night [Paul] was a man that had been with God—a man that stood high in the world and yet a man that had been lost from sight for two years. The dynamic gospel had been shut up for more than two years. No teeming crowds stood on their heads to hear him. He had not impressed anybody . . . that he was turning the world upside down. He was a jailbird, so to speak.   —C. C. Harper

These latter examples are obviously elaborations but, perhaps even more, characterizations. The Black imagination adds appropriate dimensions and details to the biblical protagonist, whether an individual or a group. It is common in Black sermons to hear lengthy and gripping discussions of Bible characters. The instinctive attempt is made to speak of the biblical person in the way one who had known him or her would speak—in the manner of one who could write of Paul, for instance, as a White House employee might write of the President, once he is out of office. In other words, the sketch is intended to be intimate, and thus more influential on the hearer, from the speaker's having been an eyewitness.

In a sermon on forgetting the things that are behind, taken from Philippians 3:13-14, I once portrayed Paul to a recently divided congregation in desperate need of forgetting many things:

I suspect that a great deal of what Paul has to say is lost to us because we are not aware of what Paul was, or *who* Paul was. Paul used to be Saul of Tarsus. He was a great scholar, a great church lawyer. He was a man of high standing and reputation, of very powerful connections. He was also a jealous defender of the faith, and he was, in fact, you might say, a murderer. For it was he who had incited the crowd to lynch Stephen. Paul was all of this, and he writes to the Philippian church and says: "I want to forget all of this. I want to forget how big a man I was. I want to forget that I was a Hebrew of the Hebrews—circumcised and all the rest." He goes on to say that he was, as touching the law, blameless, but he wants to forget even this. "I want to count all of it but dung," he says, "if I may know Christ and the power of his resurrection and the fellowship of his suffering." He is saying, "I could best use what is in the past as dung, or manure, or fertilizer, because the most important thing for me now is to know Christ." . . .

He might also have said on the same subject of forgetting that he would like to forget his sin. The Saul that was of Tarsus, the Saul that he wanted to forget, was a fiery, all out, cocksure fighter; and he was sincere—never forget it! He was *very* sincere. Yes, he led a lynch mob, but he was sincere. And he says now, "I want to forget this also." In fact, he might have said, "I don't dare think of the eyes of Stephen as he went down beneath the hail of stones. I dare not remember the look in his eyes; it would drive me crazy! I have to forget—have to *forget* what I did!"

Very relevant and typical is a characterization based on substantial imagination as well as the biblical facts. It was given by Evans Crawford, Dean of The Howard University Chapel, at the 1969 session of the Progressive National Baptist Convention. It was included in a theological lecture, which started at 10:00 P.M. and was eagerly received nevertheless. The imaginative was so well integrated with the scholarly that people who remained in the session stayed awake and involved despite the late hour. This is a great tribute both to the lecturer (who was wise enough to take lecture-depth material and cause it to sound like a sermon) and to the Black biblical tradition. Here is a transcription of parts of the characterization as taped:

You remember Moses . . . after he had committed his act of self-defense on the Egyptian taskmaster down by the brick house. You know he went away. And he went up there and he had to try to get his mind together. This is the first point, really. The responsibility of the Black church for a theology of renewal and of relevance is to work on the mind. It's in the Bible there about renewing of what? . . . the renewing of your mind! You have to get this intellectual problem all straightened out.

Now what was his problem? Don't forget. Moses was reared in the Big House. He was with the establishment, Brothers. . . . But what happened out there was that something human got him. And when they were mistreating his brother . . . he committed—just to use the language of the day—this act of self-defense. Now what happened to him? Here's what happened to him. Here was a man who had been reared in all values of the Egyptian culture. But yet he doesn't know what happened to him with that sudden act of identification. It's almost like some of you feel. . . . You don't burn, you don't loot, but you have known of so much commercial stealing that even though you will not advocate it, there's something in you that says, "Something here has got to be torn up." And so this was the kind of thing that was happening to Moses, I think. . . .

Now I'm keeping aware of the fact that this has got to be a serious discussion. And I mean it quite seriously. Moses was considering the problem of the nature of God, walking. And he was trying to get it straight, that sudden act of identification. That's what happens to people when they identify. Their whole value system gets all shaken up. Now I didn't say, when you "rationalize." I didn't say that. I said when you *identify*, the whole thing changes.

Whole groups also may be characterized imaginatively. The following description of the attitude that the church members at Jerusalem and Corinth had toward Paul is quoted from a sermon I preached on forgetting:

He was under severe suspicion, you know. When he first started preaching, they said, "That's the same fellow that used to lynch us and run us from town to town. And here he comes talking about preaching to us? Now you know that fellow ain't right! He's out to get us at ease and set us up for the kill. Then one day when we least expect, they'll chop us to death." That's what they said about Paul. After a while they got wise to the fact that this just wasn't going to be. Then they started saying other things about him. Up there at Corinth they said, "He can't preach a lick." And they said, "There's a fellow named Apollos who can preach rings around him!" And this hurt Paul; this really did. He was very sensitive about this. They said that Apollos could really preach! He could preach until the rafters rang, and Paul just couldn't begin to preach with that much power.

Paul could have gotten angry about that. But that wasn't the worst thing they said about him. You know what they were whispering around Corinth? "Girl," they were saying, "that man is crazy!" That's what they said. "This man gets caught up and he is seized by fits or something—we don't know *what's* the matter with that fellow!" And because he was aware and just couldn't be completely silent on the matter, Paul had to write in II Corinthians 5:13-14, "Whether we be beside ourselves"—in other words, if I act crazy—"it is to God; or whether we be sober, it is for your cause. For the love of Christ constraineth us."

I don't know whether Paul had epilepsy or not. Some people have tried to establish on the basis of this defensive statement that perhaps he *did* have epileptic seizures. Whatever he had, he sure had a bad name. And he didn't go off somewhere and lick his wounds and worry, and get mad when he knew that people thought there was something wrong with him. If he couldn't get to them to talk to them, he wrote them a letter, because he knew that, if you're going to serve and work with people, you can't sit around and fret. You have to go out to them and communicate. Because where two or three are gathered together, the Holy Spirit can move some of this gossip and heal relations.

Identification: The Bible as *My* Story

Another imaginative aspect of Black preaching is the choice of illustrations—gripping modern parallels to the biblical text. In the process of making the point clear, the Black experience is lifted up and celebrated, identity is enhanced, and the hearer enters vicariously into the story, making it his or her own personal story. It is just as destructive to the religious growth of Black people to use illustrations from White middle-class life as it is destructive to Black children's reading skills to have Black children reading only from White middle-class "Dick and Jane" books. The Black hermeneutic task is to interpret the gospel in terms that are readily grasped and easily identified with and appropriated.

Black translation begot Black illustration in the following transcript from a sermon I preached using parallels between Black experience and Luke 9:62:

Jesus said, "No man, having put his hand to the plough—no man that has told me that he's gonna follow me—has any business now to look back to see what happens." If you're going to plow a furrow, you can't plow it straight looking backwards. You must pick out a fencepost up on the other end of the row and plow for that mark. Don't turn your eyes, 'cause if you turn your eyes, that'll turn you *and* the mule. Anyone that puts a hand to the plow and looks back is not fit for the kingdom of heaven.

Here the typical experience of a great host of Black people with rural backgrounds not only makes them feel at home, as the gospel comes alive in terms meaningful for them, but also accurately interprets the New Testament as perhaps few other group experiences would, save that perhaps of rural Southern Whites walking the same mules down the same furrows. Jesus' world was hardly more primitive and agrarian than theirs. And because the gospel was for the people at the bottom of the totem pole, illustrations from these people's lives would automatically be nearer to the experience of the group for whom the gospel was originally written.

Black illustrations tend to stick very close to the gut issues of life and death, of struggle and frustration. And Black preachers tend to illustrate passages already chosen from the Bible on the basis of the same criteria. In the last decade of the twentieth century, White culture is prone to be concerned with other problems, but the masses of Blacks are still forced to wonder about their very survival and their ability to hold on until they receive some relief in their situation. Thus a favorite Bible passage among Blacks is interpreted with a special Black emphasis on the guarantee of God not to let the pressure (as opposed to the temptation) get too great: "But God is faithful, who will not suffer you to be tempted above that ye are able; but will with the temptation also make a way to escape, that ye may be able to bear it" (I Cor. 10:13*b*). In a favorite Black gospel song it is rendered, "He knows just how much you can bear."

The two sermon illustrations that follow are on this same text and theme, each generating great identification and appropriation.

THE SUFFERING SOUL ASKS, WHY?

Even though God doesn't get in a hurry to relieve us, he gets there on time. He gets there on time. Sometimes we don't need any particular agreement. We talk about, "Lord, if I have to bear this as long as I have, I don't know *what* I'll do." Let me tell you something: He will be there. He will be there. After every storm there are some trees that are still standing. There has been nobody yet that could determine how much you can stand. Nobody knows. Every time they come out and say that, if you get over a certain temperature or below a certain temperature-cold, you'll die. And then somebody lays out there and goes below it and *lives*. You hear them say, if a person gets to a certain pressure, you'll die. And then somebody comes along and some doctor is puzzled why this man's pressure is up there and he's walking around. Nobody knows *what* a human being can stand—nobody but God.

Sitting on my porch some years ago, I suddenly became aware that there was something going on across the street. People were hurrying, scurrying. Right away I knew that there must have been sickness in the house. I saw relatives come up, rushing in taxi cabs and automobiles. They jumped out and ran into the house and back out. And after a little while, I saw a long black automobile coming up. It got in the block. The driver looked like a man looking for a number. He drove on by the house and stopped the car, and took his time getting out, and reached in and got his coat. Everybody else was rushing, and here he was taking his time. I wondered who he was. I thought maybe he was the undertaker putting on his coat. But then he reached in and got his little bag. Then I knew who it was. That was the doctor. You see, everybody was running quickly but this man. You see, the doctor knew; from what they told him, he knew what he was going to do. And he knew that whatever was required for this case was in the bag and in his head, and so he came on up to the house leisurely strolling—knowing that he's in time.

You know, that's the way God does it. You can't hurry God—so why don't you wait, just wait. Everybody's ripping and racing and rushing. And God is taking his time. Because he knows that it isn't hurting nearly as bad as you and I think it's hurtin'—and that is the way he wants us to go. But by and by he brings relief. —Bishop A. G. Dunston

FROM OUR AWFUL DIGNITY

I preached in a certain church the other Sunday. There came down after the service a doctor who teaches in a medical school. And he came up to me, and tears came into my eyes, because I remember where he came from. He and I were born in the same town. We were born not far from a sugar plantation, and now here he was teaching at a medical college. His father and mother, I suppose, could—and I knew them—neither read nor write. And here he is now teaching at a medical college. He had gone to elementary schools where the terms were short. This doctor had battled his way—*all* of the way, I don't mean just through college, I mean from elementary school on through. Seeing him brought back faces long faded and days long passed.

Then he told me of how hard it had been for him. And how once he came home for the summer, not knowing whether he'd be able to go back to school or how he would get to the job out in the East that was promised to him. He did not have the money to get to the job. And he told me about a man, dearly loved of me, who let him have sixty-five dollars, so that he could get back to his job, so he could go to school. He said to me, "That man did not know that right then I was at the end of my courage, and if he had not given me that sixty-five dollars, I would have given up."

Now that man *did not know*—but as surely as I stand here, my faith says to me that there was somebody who *did* know, somebody who *knows* when we reach the end of our patience, somebody who *knows* when our strength has all but failed, who *knows* when we have borne the last sorrow. He is the One who cares. —Gardner C. Taylor

Storytelling

It has been clear throughout this chapter that there is much storytelling at work in the Black approach to the Bible. This is not to say that storytelling is uniquely Black, since *all* cultures love a good story. It may be more accurate to say that in America, the African American sermon is more prone to be narrative. Majority American Christianity is still coming to terms with a thing called "Narrative Theology," which leads to the expression of doctrine in stories. Even this, however, is not the folksy, natural tale-telling that moves to spiritual celebration in the African American church.

As is true of all good storytelling, the Black Bible story must first of all be a work of art in its own right. The teller must tell it as if the telling were an end in itself, though it might at times be felt that there must be interspersed asides. These point out the relevance of the story's action, which might be missed. At all times while the story is being told, the teller is caught up in it as if it had been witnessed personally. In the best tradition of the folk storyteller of all cultures, the teller must play all the roles and make the story live. Members of the audience then feel as if they too have seen the action; they participate vicariously.

Yet the story must never be told for the sake of mere entertainment. The Black preacher, like the writer of a play, has a message. Plays and stories engage the vital emotions of an audience, making possible new understanding and a fresh orientation and commitment. No matter how charming the story or how captivated the audience, the Black preacher must be about the serious business of leading the hearer to grow in some spiritual or moral way, or to increase in commitment to the Word and the kingdom of God. The response so often and freely generated by this great art form must be focused beyond the teller to the Source of the message—to God's will for the worshiper.

There was once a time when Black clergy with professional learning tended to view this folk art with suspicion, on the grounds that it was used in a manipulative way. Such concern may have had minimal warrant, but even then it was better to tell the biblical narratives in an entertaining way than to be so learned that the story never lived. Today, it is a pleasure to report that the learned Black clergy person is now trained to know the true worth of the art, and to practice it with both rigorous focus on the purposes of growth and the necessary charm to be sure it is heard. The opposite of entertaining speech is not "educational"; it is boring or obfuscating.

The most famous of all Black storytellers was John Jasper (1812–1901), founder-pastor of Sixth Mt. Zion Baptist Church in Richmond, Virginia. He was noted for moving his audiences to ecstasy with vivid views of heaven. White as well as Black crowded his gallery to be swept away with his way of making the audience *see* the Bible stories. My grandpa, who served a church in Richmond in the 1880s, was one of many Black clergy who were critical of Jasper's imaginative reconstructions and emphasis on heaven. But the proper response was not to do away with the storytelling; its power needed only to be turned to additional purposes. Meanwhile, it should be remembered that although Jasper's antebellum mentality avoided issues like civil rights, his ministry was very effective in establishing family life and essential moral qualities among the newly freed.

Jasper's sermon "De Sun Do Move" was so compelling and

popular that it was repeated quarterly to huge crowds. Here is a brief excerpt:

Let us take nex' de case uv Hezekier. He wuz one uv dem kings uv Juder. Er mighty sorry lot, I mus' say, dem kings wuz fer de mos' part. I inclines ter think Hezekier wuz 'bout de highes' in de gin'ral averig, but he wuz no mighty man hisse'f.
Well, Hezekier, he got sick. I mus' say dat a king wen he gits his crown an' fin 'ry off, an' wen he is posterated wid mortal sickness, dat he gits 'bout as common lookin', an' grunts an' rolls an' is 'bout as skeery as de res' uv us po' mortals! We know dat Hezekier wuz in a low state uv min'; full uv fears an' in a ter'ble trouble. De fac' is, de Lord strip him uv all his glory an' landed him in de dus'. He tol' him dat his hour had come, an' dat he had bettah squar' up his affairs, fer death wuz at de do'. Den it wuz dat de king fell low befo' Gord; he turn his face ter de wall; he cry, he moan, he begged de Lord not ter take him out'n de worl' yit. Oh, how good is our Gord! De cry uv de king moved His heart, an' He tell him He gwine ter give him anudder show . . .
But de Lord do even better dan dis [pity for people of low estate] fer Hezekier. He tell him He gwine ter give him a sign by which he know dat wat He sed wuz commin' ter pass. I ain't erquainted wid dem sundials dat de Lord tol' Hezekier 'bout, but ennybody dat has got a grain uv sense knows dat dey wuz de clocks uv dem ol' times an' dey mark de travels uv de sun by dem dials. Wen derefo', Gord tol' de king dat He would make de shadder go backwud, it mus' have been jes' like puttin' de han's uv de clock back; but, mark yer, Izser [Isaiah] 'spressly say dat de sun return ten dergrees. Thar yer are! Ain't dat de movement uv de sun?[5]

Eyewitness Accounts in Storytelling

This sample of John Jasper's preaching suggests a kind of intimate detail possible to storytellers who were there when it happened. These minute details are possible also to preachers who have studied and thought their way into the story so well as to visualize it rather fully. It is quite common to hear one declare, "I saw John, early one Sunday morning, on the Isle of Patmos." Everyone knows this means that he envisioned it mentally, not literally, but the result is the same: The hearer envisions the story as well. This is true also of African American culture's tales, even when they are not in a sermon or told in a church setting. R. M. Dorson, famous folklorist, was fascinated by the "insights into Negro storytelling" gained at a Negro Baptist revival in Arkansas.[6] He saw and heard spectacular sound effects and striking mimicry, and noted that many tales, told in the

71

church or in the barber shop, are told as if they were true personal experiences.

Such eyewitness accounts establish folk characterizations that are convincingly detailed and life-scale. The natural response is to feel as if "I *know* that fellow!" The character may come from the early Old Testament, but the visceral response is that "I have known that lady ever since I was a kid." The late Sandy F. Ray must have had thousands of these people with whom to make sermon events into real-life encounters. At a large convention I heard a characterization that was better than the big screen in living color.

We recognize that the disciples were pushing for power. They had had people lording over them all their lives—they had been bossed all of their days. And now they wanted to be bosses themselves. Jesus sensed that several times. On one occasion people were disputing over who was going to be boss—who was going to be the head person when he came into his empire. They thought they could see that he was moving towards becoming king, and they were getting ready. They wanted to be assigned as officials in the empire. Who was going to be head?

There was a very dedicated woman, you remember, who went to him because she had two sons—like Brother Williams here has two fine sons. And she went to Jesus and said, "Look, Jesus, when you come into your kingdom—when you get into your power—I want to talk to you now, because I know it is going to be rushed and mean after you get in. There'll be lots of folks pushing and shoving. But I want to get to you now, because you know my sons—you know me and you know my sons. You know I've dedicated them. . . . When we get into the kingdom, Sir, let one of my sons sit on the right hand and the other on the left."[7]

The teller gave the impression that he was moving effortlessly among numberless remembered details, from which he had selected the proper ones, to avoid cluttering up the characterization unnecessarily. Without seeing the mother's face or hair or height, one saw her typical motherly concern to ensure that her children would get ahead in the world. We *all* knew that woman, maybe the head of the women's society at our home church, and we were ready for the punch line about power when Dr. Ray delivered it.

The Universal Bible

It must be obvious by now that this approach to the Bible has universal appeal. In a day when there is great need to restore the

Bible to the center of life and culture, there is no better way to accomplish the task than through the memory of stories. It has the charm of folk culture and the purposeful sophistication of the best of scholarship, whether based on formal study or natural genius. Of course, the truth is that Blacks have never had a monopoly on this approach in the first place. There have always been Whites and persons of other races who did it the same way; they simply haven't been dominant in their culture. A classic example is Clarence Jordan (1912–1969), founder-leader of the Koinonia Farm, an experimental Christian community with raceless working and living patterns, in southwest Georgia. His Ph.D. in New Testament Greek was used to "translate" the Bible into the earthy, sweaty language of his often quite hostile White neighbors. His stories were powerfully contemporary, although they did not share with the Black approach the insistence on a powerful sermonic celebration at the end. Here is one translation, transcribed from a sound recording, best received if "listened to" in his Georgia accent while one reads:

Jesus told a story one time, of a very rich man who liked to give a big party and invite in a lot of his cronies and serve them mint juleps out under his big magnolia trees, and just be the real aristocratic old gentleman with his goatee and his pince-nez glasses, a very cultured fellow. And all the while he was putting on this party there was laid at his gate a poor man named Lazarus. Now the rich man never did like to see this poor fellow around; he always said, "My, he's so awful looking, and he isn't even my color, and he's dirty and filthy, and I wish I didn't have him hanging around me so much."

He got the idea that he would build a big, high, woven-wire fence around his place, so that when he had a party he could lock the gate and not let any of those unsightly beggars be around asking him for bread, and draining his mint julep glasses. So he built that kind of a fence and enjoyed his privacy for a number of years.

But in due time the poor man, the beggar, died and was carried away to the other world. Also the rich man, as all rich men do, died and was carried away to the other world. It so happened that in this other life, things were completely reversed. The man who had been begging for bread found that he had plenty of bread. The poor beggar, Lazarus, who was so lacking in friends, now found that he had plenty of friends. And Lazarus, who had been so ostracized and segregated, now found that he was in the fellowship of all of the people of God, among whom was the great old patriarch of the race, Abraham himself. And many a time Abraham would invite old Lazarus over to his house for an evening banquet of fried chicken, black-eyed peas, gravy, rice, and collard greens.

Now it so happened that the rich man found that he no longer had his table set with all the dainties and delicacies of the South. He found that he didn't

73

even have a drink of water, and the temperature was unseasonably hot, and getting even worse, along with extremely high humidity. And in this rather parched state, the rich man said, "Ooh I wonder where my water boy is. *Boy!* Bring me some water!" And no boy comes. And finally, he sees this old beggar that had peered through the woven-wire fence back on earth, with his hungry look, wanting a little bit of bread—he sees him over there at the table with all kinds of water, and Pepsi Colas, and cool drinks and everything, and he cries out to Mr. Abraham, "Please, would you send that boy over here with some water to rub over my tongue, because I am in deep agony in this high heat and high humidity."

Well, Mr. Abraham says to him, "You know, while you were alive you had all the good things; you had the good sections of town; you had the good streets; you had the good schools; you had the good political offices; you had the good income, and Lazarus had to take what was left. He just got the scraps when you got through. He got the sections of town that you didn't want; he got the streets that you no longer used. You shut him out, and he had to take what was left. Now it happens that things have been completely reversed; you are hungry and thirsty, and he is well fed and well watered. But the big problem is that there has been a big gulf dug between us and you, a *deep* ditch. Now I want to remind you that that ditch is as deep here as your fence was high on earth, and it's just as impenetrable. We can't cross this deep ditch which you dug to keep men like Lazarus out—you wanted to segregate him, you didn't want him around. You were successful; you shut him out; and now you want him to cross over—but there's no bridge, just a deep ditch, and he can't get to you with the water to cool your tongue. Nor can you come to us, because you know when you dig a ditch it breaks up traffic both ways. He can't come to you, and you can't come to us; you'll have to continue in your torment, which is your doing."

Well one good thing about this old, rich fellow, he did realize and was willing to confess his guilt. He said, "You know I have some brothers back there that are thinking just like I thought; they've got the same notions that I had. Would you please—since Lazarus can't come to me—would you please let him go back to earth to my brothers down there, and tell them how awful it is to break communications, how awful it is to dig gulfs between themselves and their fellowman, so that they won't come to this stage of torment that I'm in."

And Abraham says, "Well, those people down there, they got the Baptist churches and the Methodist churches and the Presbyterian churches and the Episcopalian churches. They got the preachers; they got the Bible. They got the freedom of assembly; they got the freedom of speech. Let them listen to the Bible, and let them listen to the preachers, and let them do what the churches teach them to do."

And this fellow says, "Oh no, they won't listen to the Bible; they won't listen to the preachers, but if you'll let Lazarus go back there and kinda scare the daylights out of them, maybe along late one Saturday night, I believe you'll get some action out of them. But they ain't going to listen to these preachers."

74

And Abraham says, "Well if they won't be persuaded to do right by the preachers and by the word of God, they won't be persuaded even though somebody goes to them from the dead."[8]

Clarence Jordan was not popular in southwest Georgia. Crosses were burned on his community's farm, and they even burned his buildings. But he made real inroads into the life of his time and place. Today his influence is felt all over the world in a program originated at Koinonia; it is called Habitat for Humanity.

The universal appeal of the Black approach to the Bible is perhaps best evident in the nationwide popularity of Samuel D. Proctor. He too is a Ph.D., with two college presidencies, years as a very distinguished professor, and concurrent years as pastor of a great church. But with all his attractive learning, he has never lost his marvelous gift for telling stories, learned in his early years in Virginia. He can really tell a Bible story, and his preaching always offers hope and great wisdom. Bill Moyers, network news commentator and former Peace Corps administrator, wrote the foreword for Dr. Proctor's recent book. In the foreword, he hailed him as America's most popular commencement speaker. "Reliable sources tell me that Sam Proctor will deliver more graduate speeches than any other person in the country. Actually, Sam does not just speak. He preaches. Oh, my, how he preaches. He is a born preacher."[9] And we might add that his approach to the Bible, with all his learning and warmth, is an important ingredient of that widely sought preaching.

CHAPTER 5

Preaching
and the Mother Tongue
of the Spirit

By far the most controversial chapter in the first edition of *Black Preaching* was entitled "Black English." Old and dear friends took issue with me, and classes still have trouble dealing with the very existence of a system of communication which is actually unique to the African American communities. On the other hand, two nationally distributed textbooks on communication printed the chapter in toto, and many more articles and journals took this chapter for law and gospel. In the community of linguists, a rather precise professional body, the final word had been spoken by an ethnic from within. The chapter stays—and is presented here following a brief introduction—with the changes and improvements that come with the twenty years since it was first published.

The problem is not one of accuracy or acceptability, but of understanding. And the understanding is desperately needed, since so much hangs on the ability to communicate with persons where their spirituality is deepest. Most Americans practice religion in their native language, with its own experiential frame of reference, its own visual images, and its own typical sounds and choice of vocabulary. (Dialect is least important.) In other words, people's faith is naturally expressed in their mother tongue—the language, be it English or something else, into which they were born.

A good example of this is the lunch I attended in a Hispanic home in San Jose, California, where the pastor-host wanted me to meet his gifted son. This honor student in aeronautical engineering was flawless in English, but when we bowed to say grace, he burst forth,

"Padre nuestra, que estas en los cielos. . . ." It was the Lord's Prayer, in Spanish. Much later in the day I teased him a bit: "¿Que pasa? ¿Dios no habla la lengua ingles?" (What's the matter? Doesn't God speak English?) The minute I said it I recognized my error. I should never have embarrassed him about the fact that his faith was in the language in which he had worshiped all his life. So is everybody else's faith, unless there is a concentrated exposure or effort toward change.

I saw this truth clearly for the first time that day, but I was to learn it under much harder circumstances. I was completing a master's degree in linguistics, for which the research required hundreds of hours of listening to tapes of the best of Black preaching. Unbeknown to me, I began to sound like my models, all of whom had been reared in the South, with all the softer sounds that this implies. Before this time, I had sounded like what I was born, a Midwesterner with the "standard" American accent—the language of the middle class and my birthplace. It was also the language of the national media, but it was heard among many of my congregation as the language of the oppressor. Although they weren't aware of the difference, it was not the language of their religious experience. I found out how they felt when they shared their comments: "Reverend Mitchell, we thought you would get worse when you went back to school, but you surprised us. You're really letting the Lord use you now!" This meant that with all my earlier effort and commitment, I had come through as resisting the Lord in the pulpit.

This reaction to an unconscious shift in style was repeated all over the area where I had served for fourteen years. Some even went so far as to hazard a guess that I had finally gotten religion. All of this meant that the hundreds of sermons preached over that six-hundred-mile-long territory had been merely tolerated; the invitation to preach was a way of saying thanks for services rendered, not a response to my efforts to proclaim the Word. The difference was not in my prayer life or preparation habits; it was in the very subtle, providential ways my tongue had evolved from crisp standard English to the sounds of those preachers on tape, not one of whom had a glaringly Southern dialect.

The difference was also in a combination of images and sounds, which had crept into and blessed my preachment to the vast majority of the African Americans whom I sought to serve. The only complaints I heard were from a few college students and graduates, who sensed something different and thought it was a false move on my part. There was further opposition when I conducted workshops for school districts on the subject of linguistic difference as an index to social distance and teacher-pupil rapport. Many Black teachers had struggled so hard to "speak proper English" that they resented deeply my suggestion that they retain some of their native tongue with which to establish identity with their students.

There is a science of how identity is associated with the typical sounds and vocabulary of various regions, classes, professions, and ethnic or cultural groups.[1] The identity established by sound takes precedence over the identity suggested by appearance, so Black preachers don't have to *look* Black to communicate if they can *sound* as if they belong. An old man can really reach youth by just using their code words. For these realizations I am indeed grateful. One of my favorite passages of Scripture is Paul's claim to being multiculturally competent, by means of identification (I Cor. 9:19-22):

For though I be free from all men, yet have I made myself servant unto all, that I might gain the more. And unto the Jews I became as a Jew, that I might gain the Jews . . . to them that are without law, as without law, . . . that I might gain them that are without law. To the weak became I as weak, that I might gain the weak. I am made all things to all men, that I might by all means save some.

With this ideal of a multilingual preacher who can establish rapport with a multiplicity of identities in mind, let us turn now to what was a controversial chapter.

* * *

Black preaching requires the use of Black language—the rich rendition of English spoken in the Black ghetto. To many Americans, of whatever color, such an assertion may cause some consternation. Speakers will ask, "Do you want me to say 'dis and dat'?" or "Must I unlearn all my learning and talk 'flat'?" This raises three important questions: (1) Why Black English in the first place? (2) How is it learned? and (3) What is Black English anyway? I shall try to resolve them in the order given.

Why Black English in the First Place?

The not-very-well-known fact about all spoken English is that there is no one universally accepted or "proper" version. "Standard" American English, to the extent that there is a version more generally accepted than others, is probably a North-Midland White, middle-class variety of English. Every other region of the United States will have its own variant of this speech standard, even within the same middle-class White majority. Every ethnic group or regional subculture will have its variants, each peculiarly conditioned by the influences of history, geography, social class, and the like.

Such groups are sometimes referred to as speech communities. Within such a speech community it is easiest to communicate by using the patterns of that group. The subtle meaning and shades of meaning, the particular pronunciation and accent, the intonation and entire signal system of any given group are altogether "proper" to that group. In fact, no language is improper among its users, since it alone is most capable of the task for which all language exists: communication.

This rule is especially meaningful to missionaries in foreign lands, who take great care to learn the communication system of the people among whom they are to serve. In America, however, a diabolical combination of racism, class snobbery, and naivete has caused Blacks as well as Whites to assume, consciously or unconsciously, that there is a single proper American English, and that the language spoken by most Black people is a crude distortion of it. In religious circles, standard White middle-class English is assumed to be the only vehicle for the preaching of the gospel and the praising of the Lord in public. The results have been rather disastrous for the church of the Black masses, because the vast majority of Black-culture churches have found it difficult to understand or relate to trained Black clergy persons preaching Whitese to them. Consequently, those few trained Blacks who are also fluent in Black English—the language of their people—have been conspicuously effective and in greater demand.

Trained Black clergy have had to be, for the most part, proficient in White culture in order to satisfy college and seminary requirements. American colleges and seminaries have been heavily influenced by the not-so-subtle assumption that "White is right," especially their

79

White, middle-class culture and its version of the English language.

The result is that, whenever a substantial number of Black-culture churches have been faced with the choice between a preacher who can communicate with them or one who is seminary trained, they have chosen communication over education. In fact, it has often been argued by the faithful that those preachers who obviously strive to preach "proper" to their Black congregations are possibly not even "saved." The sincerest efforts of trained men to relate themselves to the Black-ghetto church have accordingly been all too often misunderstood. Their efforts have been tainted by their unconscious lack of the cultural identity so crucial to deep communication. To refuse to learn and use the people's language is an affront to the people one presumes to serve. The new breed of truly educated Black clergy have been lately alerted to the subtleties of this impasse, and they are doing something about it. While it may still be embarrassing to the educated Black seminarian, who is still trapped in the culture of the academy, it is rewarding for others who have learned to come to terms with their heritage to have it whispered around the church that the educated pastor is also filled with the Spirit.

On the other hand, some Black churches have pastors whose fluency and competence are limited to the Black idiom. Sensing their limitations, such pastors often avoid contact beyond their home churches and their own culture. As a result, their churches may forfeit involvement in issues or programs relevant to many needs of Blacks today. Their limited effectiveness creates a vacuum or a distortion in ghetto leadership. The Black church then becomes isolated from the larger community for which it should be an important resource.

One answer to this problem lies in teaching pastors who are already fluent in Black exposition to be at home in standard English, so that they can increase their capabilities to deal with issues. Another answer lies in the teaching of Black language and religious culture to the professionally trained Black clergy, who may then make more effective use of their training and deal more effectively with the needs of the Black masses and the issues affecting their well-being. Still a third answer lies in the recruitment of able Black-culture-oriented candidates for training in the seminaries, taking care to avoid brainwashing them or stripping them of their original culture. All too many theological seminaries were once in the habit of molding Blacks into a White image and sending them out to serve Black people in Black churches. And this unfortunate practice was not limited to White majority seminaries. Happily, the bias of these seminaries is diminishing, and a new generation of Black students is being urged to discover the riches of being what they are—Black.

The question will no doubt arise about why the church is not used to promote standard culture and "lift" the Black masses into the mainstream of American culture and its benefits. The answer is very simple: No free Black-culture church will ever call a pastor who cannot speak the language of its people. To expect them to become bicultural may be realistic. But to expect them to learn their cultural duality from a (Black) White person is absurd. Neither faith nor culture will be communicated by a preacher whose language sounds to the ghetto resident as if he or she is putting on airs, for implicit in this seeming posturing is a deprecation of the very people to be served. The church will reject the preacher summarily if cultural indexes suggest a fundamental loyalty to a White reference group rather than to their religious culture.

Seminary-trained Blacks must be models of all things to all people, helping the cultures to come closer together by being instruments of translation of each to the other. They must be fluent in Black language, for this is fundamental to their calling, and yet they must also be fluent in standard English, because they must communicate beyond the congregation. Their language must be Black enough to generate rapport with the congregation by means of an identity which is perceived as close. They must be able to touch the souls of Black folk with soul language, putting them at ease and gaining greatest access by avoiding the linguistic signals of social distance. Yet they must also be able to reinforce and keep alive the "standard" learnings of the young people of the congregation, which link them to the larger community. It must be clear to the congregation that the pastor isn't limited to Black language, so that they will have confidence that the pastor can adequately represent their interests outside the ghetto.

This type of bilingual skill has been resisted by middle-class teachers in the Black ghetto, on the grounds that it is phony and seems to make fun of the ghetto culture—as an Amos-and-Andy set of mannerisms. If Black language were suggested as the sole vehicle of spoken communication, then of course the protesting teachers would seem to have a point. Even so, Black language is far more than an ignorant jumble of unaspirated mumbling. It is the lingua franca of the Black ghetto, full of subtle shadings of sound and significance, cadences and color. It beguiles the hearers because it is familiar. It establishes rapport and influence with them, without their being conscious of the fact that the preacher has deliberately chosen this language as the most appropriate to the task of meaningful communication. This is one of the chief skills of Black preachers who are effective and charismatic, despite their professional training. The cadences of the late Dr. Martin Luther King, Jr., were unashamedly Black. His learning could be used to lead the Black masses because he was always heard as a soul brother.

How Is Black English Learned?

Before offering some technical description and analysis of the Black language presently in wide use, I should perhaps explain, as far as possible, how this language is learned. All languages are learned best by living and identifying with the people who speak them. In a sense, one must for a time burn one's bridges and identify closely with the target culture group. When this is done, the nuances will be learned subconsciously. Thus children reproduce the speech of those socially closest to them (family and peer group) rather than those whom they may hear most—for example, teacher or television. Should the family change neighborhoods and encounter a difference between their speech and the speech of the child's new playmates, the child's choice of identity will be subconsciously decided, but that choice will become evident through speech patterns. Preachers who grew up with White speech will best learn Black speech after overcoming some of the subtle vestiges of the White self-identity that went with the White tongue. Of course they may need to retain at least some whiteness to be truly bicultural and bilingual. But if they are to talk Black and hope to reach Blacks effectively, Blacks will have to become persons of primarily Black identity.

Given an acceptance and appreciation of Black identity, one's ear is attuned to the sounds of one's parents, and one's tongue consciously and subconsciously shapes its own sounds to avoid contrast with those to whom one feels closest. The more unconscious and therefore not self-conscious the Black utterance is, the better the possibilities of accurate communication.

Black preachers might well devise a range of situations in which they employ degrees of Blackness in utterance. For example, a sermon or a conversation might include a quote of extremely Black speech in a way that does not ridicule the original speaker and, in fact, interprets that person more accurately. In another situation, one might deal rather analytically with a matter in the pure standard dialect. In still another situation, one might paraphrase a verse of scripture. For instance, a Black preacher could render God's speech to Peter in the text against racism (Acts 10:14-15) thus: "Looka here, Peter, don't you be callin' *nothin'* I made common or dirty!"

To grasp this rendering, the preacher requires the Black intonation and accent so necessary to the complete Black signal system, but the authentic Blackness of such a translation must, in some measure, come through on even the black and white of this paper. This paraphrase-translation has several important advantages. In the first place it presents the message in a familiar and authentic folk-art form, and it attracts attention by giving pleasure and making folks at home, or comfortable. Second, it reinforces and supports Black identity by putting in the mouth of God the language of the people. In White-language preaching, this highly important emotional support is reserved for members of the White-speech community. No Black person can truly identify with a God who speaks only the language of the White oppressor. A Black rendition of scripture does in language what a Black Christ or a Black Madonna does in art; God is divested of a "proper," White, socially distant image. The personification of deity is no longer completely outside Black life and culture. Just how great is this need for reidentification of God with Black people can be seen in the words of the prayer by a faithful Black deacon: "If your blue eyes in glory find anything wrong in this place . . ." Finally, the message is made much more understandable by the use of familiar language. The lesson of the message is better learned because the biblical scene is vicariously experienced in the worship, rather than simply heard in theory. This experiential factor is greatly reduced when the message is offered in a distant tongue.

The progress here discussed is parallel to the changes of language and image now being made in textbooks for Black ghetto schools across the nation. Just as the language of the "Dick and Jane" readers gets minimal response from the Black-ghetto child and has therefore to be discarded, so must complete dependence on White middle-class language be discarded in favor of an indigenous Black mix of languages, and for the same reasons. In fact, if a preacher uses standard English exclusively, with no Black sounds and shadings, the chances of being asked back to a Black-culture church are very slim. It is no exaggeration to say that the chances of being called to serve such a church are virtually nil. The rejection of the preacher will not be a rejection of the education per se, but a resistance to the imposition of an alien culture on the only institution that is Black owned and Black controlled, and can therefore insist on being led by a Black pastor.

What Is Black English?

What then are the contrasting features that distinguish Black English from standard English? One is the slower rate of delivery. Another is Black sentence structure, which on the average is simpler than typical middle-class sentence structure. Still other differences range all the way from highly technical and subtle usages down to the various local tonal inflections characteristic of some Southern Blacks. As I have said, no book about these features of speech could teach one to use them effectively. The best a book can do is to hint at them. Only a healthy Black identity, born of acute exposure to the Black experience and of complete Black self-acceptance, can complete the process of lingual identification and implant Black language naturally on one's tongue. (For these reasons, many Black social workers are now avoiding the placement of a Black child among White adoptive parents.)

Perhaps the most common feature stereotypically associated with Black speech is the "down home" drawl, which must not be confused with the White Southern drawl from the same region. The Black drawl has its own special kind of "flatness," a word denoting lazily articulated vowels and consonants, and imprecise closure or dropped word endings. This description must not be taken as a White-standard judgment against Black language or culture. It is simply a fact that the word *lazy* applies to both Black and White Southern pronunciation of the long vowel "I." It is composed of "ah" and "ee," and both give only the first part. Whites probably drop it more than Blacks, either North or South. In fact, the first Black president of the United States will probably have to sound much more standard on his long "I" vowels than did the first president from Texas, who was White.

If one can forget the negative connotations of "lazy" speech, then one can sense that soft, velvet sounds are much more able to communicate warmth and to avoid harsh overtones. Few can deny the charm of a drawl. Many Southern Whites go so far as to consider it an identity signal of Southern aristocracy. Whatever fear Blacks may have had of a drawl, as used by Whites, has been conditioned not by the sound itself but by the racist treatment that all too often has gone with it. In a word, the softened consonants have universal advantage and signal value in the Black speech community. The degree of softening may vary greatly, but Blackese is surely not characterized by the crisp consonants so common in my formerly Midwestern speech.

A full-fledged drawl, however, is not by any means a universal characteristic of Black speech. Nor is another feature: unmatched subjects and verbs. This failure of agreement is called bad grammar within the standard middle-class communication system. But the word "bad" must never be used by one culture regarding another. No language is bad that conveys adequately the intended meaning to the intended audience. "Ungrammatical" is a less judgmental term, but it still implies that there is one standard form, by which all others are judged. Among Blacks of the ghetto, the speaker does not have to say "you is" to be accepted, but the speaker is certainly permitted to say it if he or she wishes, and some will not hear anything unusual in it. "You is" and "you are" are both permitted in the Black American mother tongue.

Much good communication takes place in Black culture without such extreme contrasts with standard language as "You is." One can be quite Black and still use neither a drawl nor such grammar as "He play the piano." Perhaps the most important thing is that a Black-culture person hears departures from standard English and has no great urge to correct them, because all desire to please the ruling majority with one's speech has been lost. So-called standard language is only the speech of those in power in a given place; there is no salvation in it, only a better job perhaps. In the preaching event, there is no such need to hold to a strict adherence to standard.

Another interesting contrast between Blackese and standard speech is in the different uses to which Blacks put function words or prepositions. When one says in Blackese "I got sick behind it," one means after it in time and not behind it in space. Blacks sang "Freedom over Me" in slavery days, and young Blacks popularized the slave song in the sit-in era, but the word "over" designated no relationship normally associated with the preposition "over" in standard speech. Then there is the common Black statement "I'm gonna go up side your head." It means, "I'm going to hit you on the head." It implies two prepositions, "up" and "beside," but here again is a wide and common departure from standard usage. A final illustration is the word "around." To "mess around" is colloquial for aimless and nonproductive activity. But in Blackese the usage is altered to give the verb "mess" a direct object, using "around," thus, in a Black complaint, "You messed me 'round."

Another common contrast with standard English involves archaic English and logical but ungrammatical constructions. One of these is quoted above in God's response to Peter. "Don't you be callin'" is a logical combination, but the grammatical or accepted way to say it is "Don't you dare call." This same irregular verb "to be" is treated by Blacks as a regular verb, and a report on a person's condition may be rendered "He be's all right." An archaic pronunciation of the auxiliary verb "might" survives in a common response in Black lodge ritual as they intone, "So mote it be." And it survives as "mought" (rhymes with out) in the conversation of Blacks from Virginia and North Carolina. Blacks also use words like "fetch," "tote," "holp" (for "help"), and "yonder," to a greater extent than other groups. But all these usages can be found among Whites, particularly those from Appalachia.

It may be argued on the basis of this shared vocabulary that language differences are regional rather than racial. But, as has been pointed out already, there is a considerable difference between White Southern dialect and Blackese. Regional influences will indeed be shared between Black and White, but the principal influence on Black culture and language is the Black experience, and this is not shared with Whites. Blacks live in another world from that of the Whites of the same Southern city. And the racial aspect of cultural difference only increases in the North, where White Southerners are assimilated or at least distributed, and Blacks from the South are huddled together to cling to their beleaguered dignity and their mother tongue. Blackese means far more to a Northern-born resident of the ghetto than Southernese would mean to an ex-Southern White, simply because the White can be fully as-similated and the Black cannot.

Even with the easy adjustment of Whites among Whites, however, the rule still holds that all people love to hear their mother tongue. This is illustrated by the popularity among Whites of Country and Western music, a part of whose charm is the dialect. Migrant Whites, the affluent as well as the deprived, like to hear the way people spoke "when I was a kid." Blacks whose natural tastes have not been destroyed will follow this rule also. The native language is comforting to all who have not denied their roots and identity.

It is not mandatory that a Black use this language, but it never hurts in the effort to communicate. A Black English teacher in a high school once told me of a noisy back row of Blacks who simply would not join the class. When she departed from the script and sternly ordered, "Hush! Y'all ain't talkin' 'bout nothin'!" they sat up and took notice. This was her opening wedge of effective communication; she had declared with her language that she was willing to be one of them and therefore was to be respected.

This indicates something very significant for educated Black clergy about how to be linguistically flexible, in order to communicate with most of the congregation at most times and in most circumstances. Especially in times of crisis, people do not hear well the words of a stranger, spoken in a foreign tongue. To communicate effectively, Black preachers have to adjust their language to a variety of settings and offer many shadings within the two basic cultures, Black and White. The most crucial of these settings is the Black pulpit, and the most demanding culture for these purposes is African American or Black. The day will undoubtedly come when the barriers have fallen to the extent that there is virtually one tongue. In the meanwhile we do well to establish a variety of tongues, being certain that one of them speaks to the spirit of the masses. Although this mother tongue may never be formally committed to print, and though it should probably not be taught in the schools, it still speaks to the depths of many, and it still declares that the preacher or speaker is willing to be counted among the number whose native tongue it still is.

CHAPTER 6

Personal Style
in Black Preaching

From its earliest beginnings, Black preaching has been clearly
characterized by the affirmation of authentic personal mannerisms. About the most certain statement one can make regarding
Black preaching style is that no pattern is rigidly established. Black
preachers range all the way from those known to proclaim the gospel
from ladders and coffins and in other spectacular ways, to others
noted for standing "flatfooted" (in one place) and hardly raising their
voices, while stirring large audiences. In between is a vast array of
mannerisms, styles, and approaches well worth reviewing, both
because of human interest and because of their importance as part of
the Good News incarnate. Such liberty in the Spirit exemplifies the
liberation preached to the oppressed in the Black church.

The Use of Mannerisms

The first thing that must be said about peculiarities of style is that
the Black congregation is very permissive. It accepts a considerable
variety of behavior unrelated to the message, in order (consciously or
unconsciously) to free preachers to be themselves. One preacher in
wide demand among Blacks and Whites popped his suspenders when
he was really caught up in his message. Another unbuttoned his
collar and seemed to dig his chin into his chest. One preacher cried
and seemed to wail her words when the Spirit was high. Still another
used a patented exclamation, "Bless my bones!" Yet another used to
start his sermons only after an unbelievably long, intense, and even

stern glare at the congregation. It would be surprising to hear a complaint against any of these, no matter how unusual the behavior might be in another setting.

Black-culture Christians generally enjoy mannerisms, provided they are natural and not overworked. Mannerisms add interest and signal a freedom and authentic personhood in which the congregation participates vicariously, by identification. The preacher is not actually required to devise a trademark in order to be accounted authentically Black, but it is certainly not a handicap if one happens to engage in uniquely colorful pulpit habits. A preacher's individuality is celebrated, and acceptance is communicated by the hearers with audible and visible responses enjoyed by both preacher and hearer.

The Use of Tone

In addition to mannerisms, Black preachers abound in other stylistic features. The most common or stereotypical is the use of a musical tone or chant in preaching. Among initiates it is variously referred to as "moaning," "whooping," "tuning," "zooning," or any one of several other more localized terms, each with a slightly different shade of meaning.

Sustained tone is used in various ways. The most widely sought Black preachers in the country tend to use intonation only in climactic utterance, or celebration, if they use it at all. Others, because of the traditions of their background, tend to use some degree of tone throughout the message. In between, the decision is formed on the basis of a combination of factors: the preacher's vocal capabilities, the expectations and responses of the hearers in a particular congregation, and the preacher's personal identification with the material in the sermon. The decision will often be made unconsciously, just as a truck driver adjusts his gears to the grades of the road. Yet most churches no longer demand tonality, if indeed they ever did. Thus the precise present significance of this feature is very difficult to assess.

It is a fact that it automatically makes some folks "happy" just to hear the tonal aspect of their religious mother tongue sounded in the pulpit. For people with a certain background, it appears that a moaned message is more deeply spiritual than an unintoned one. Although this is not necessarily true, tone does signal a kind of affirmation of Black identity which is often used of the Holy Spirit as the catalyst for a deep religious experience. Another way to say it would be that for many older Blacks their first religious experience came with intoned preaching; thereafter, the response became more and more conditioned, so that any preacher using such a technique would automatically get a greater response simply by this association.

Historically speaking, intonation as a factor in Black preaching style no doubt stems from the fact that African languages tend to use tonal qualities as a part of the signal system. What is more, the history of much of Black Africa was preserved, in the absence of writing, in song, as were its laws, customs, and traditional folk stories and hero tales. There were also highly spontaneous or impromptu songs for various life situations, such as the voicing of grievances. And there were folktales or fables of wisdom and morality, for guidance in life's problems.[1] This understanding of history and anthropology adds much to the accuracy of our knowledge of the very first Negro spirituals, as contrasted with those edited and published later. It also explains why early Black peddlers (and some to this day) sold ice, coal, fish, and vegetables with street-chanted sales talks. It suggests, too, why eighteenth-century Blacks thronged to hear the sonorous musicality of George Whitefield in the First Great Awakening.[2] What once took the place of print in African culture stayed on to serve Blacks in other ways. It first reminded them of home, and later it was simply something they had to themselves, not shared or understood or controlled by Whites. It was an affirmation of Black identity, a means of celebrating and supporting Black personhood.

While intonation has general significance as an identity signal, it has certainly come to be used widely by Black preachers to indicate celebration. Yet intonation seems seldom to be taken seriously by acknowledged leaders of the Black pulpit, as indicated by a study of tapes of Black preaching I conducted. Only a few preachers on the tapes seemed really to depend on intonation. In more than half of the sermons, the moaning climax was not sustained, nor apparently was it important. In fact, although three fourths of the more widely known preachers I studied used at least some form of intonation in their celebrations, a highly significant minority of equal impact used nothing of the sort. Furthermore, I found that while some of these speakers did not use intonation on any of the tapes in my collection, they did use it on other occasions.

This study made readily apparent that many Black congregations no longer require intonation for a religiously celebrative experience. The more universal factor seemed to be a choice of celebrative material. Some of this amounted to old, well-worn climax cliches. Among the preachers whom I considered the better ones, celebration material tended to be related to the solid content of the message, and at the same time inherently moving, as well as movingly presented.

Perhaps the most important thing that can be said about intonation is that it can never be used effectively unless it is part of the natural style or language of the speaker. To use it insincerely, as an easy means of access and manipulation, is to run the risk of failure as well as to belittle and degrade the Black preaching tradition. But it should also be said that wherever pastors or congregations frown on and arbitrarily repress this common feature of Black religious culture, the worship is in danger of no longer being in the idiom of the Black masses. In Black worship, the congregation's warm acceptance of any sincere expression of the Black experience must be taken for granted.

There are, however, exceptions. Many churches in the towns and the countryside of Virginia, for instance, are quite content without intonation. They are truly of the masses, but they have grown a little tired or suspicious of the preachers they have heard use "whooping," perhaps to excess. One member of a pulpit committee said she was pleased with a brilliant graduating senior whom I had sent to preach as a candidate at her church. As she put it, "He preaches a wonderful sermon, but why does he always have to chase that little bear at the end?" By that she meant that his celebrations were always intoned. That strong, semirural church called another candidate.

The Use of Rhythm

Closely associated with the stereotypical use of intonation by Black preachers is the use of rhythm in preaching. Most White observers, including folklorists, anthropologists, and theologians, never seem to be able to discover the one without the other. My own observations during fifty years in the pulpit, as well as my study of taped sermons, however, would seem to support the idea very little that Black preachers use rhythm to any great degree. The most that could be said about the majority of preachers I have studied is that lengthy intonation requires breaks for breath! In many cases, this makes room for response, but it does not seem to follow any poetic or musical beat or meter.

Since I completed the study of tapes previously mentioned, some twenty-five years ago, an exception has evolved: organ accompaniment to the sermonic celebration. At times this can influence the preacher to move in the direction of rhythmic meter, engaged in spontaneously. All too often it is the brainchild of the musician. And just as often it is hardly to be thought of as a legitimate offspring of the African American pulpit tradition. More appropriate may be the accusation that it is the child of Hollywood and the media.

It would be safe to say that modern Black worshipers do not require or expect any special pattern of rhythm. If a Black preacher happens to have a rhythmic singsong delivery, it is, like other features, warmly accepted so long as it appears sincere. For a few, rhythm may be a pleasant reminder of older days when it may have been much more common. Among some groups it is used for a mass rhythmic experience, which may or may not be truly religious. For the rest, my studies would seem to indicate that, while rhythm is vital to Black music, it is, to say the least, not very important in Black preaching.

The Use of Call and Response and Repetition

A far more important feature, implied in the consideration of rhythm, is the call and response. Many preachers who pause momentarily to breathe or for other reasons receive a response from the audience. When a Black preacher quotes the centurion (Matt. 27:54), it is almost obligatory that a pause follow the first "truly," to provide the congregation time to repeat the word. In fact, this may be done several times before the quotation (which is excellent for the celebration) is completed with "this was the Son of God." This pattern has roots deep in Black African culture.

The Black preacher who is still uneasy and inhibited about such elements as the call and response should remember that even the structured worship of the liturgical churches gives people a place to respond in the collects or series of prayers. How much better, then, for purposes of Black worship, to provide in the sermon a place where Black people can express themselves or unburden their hearts with a "Have Mercy!" or "Truly!" or "Early!" Here is genuine, happy, satisfying dialogue with the preacher. Nowhere is there a better example of the audience participation now so suddenly treasured, in theory at least, by today's liturgists. (Audience participation is so important that chapter 7 is devoted to it.)

In truly Black preaching, repetition occurs not only in the call and response, but also in the normal course of the sermon. Texts, aphorisms, and other significant statements are restated for emphasis, memory, impact, and effect. The Black audience takes the gospel seriously and does not feel "talked down to" when words or sentences are repeated. Not uncommonly, the repetition is so vivid that it may be heard again in later conversation, days after it was given life in the pulpit. If the gospel is indeed the word of life, then ought it not to include nuggets worth repeating the next day or the next year? Black preaching assumes that things need time to sink in. The emphasis is on intensity of response and not extensity of material covered. What in another context might seem pompous becomes meaningful in the Black congregation where repetition has a completely different connotation.

The Use of Role Playing and Storytelling

Black preachers, like any others, risk pomposity when they assume roles in their speaking—such as the role of God or some character or spectator in a Bible narrative—but a role carefully portrayed is a tremendous asset to preaching. Whatever the role or multiplicity of roles assumed, it adds immeasurably to the impact and worth of the story. The Black preacher who is so "siditty"[3] as to preach always in the third person is clearly not of Black culture—and is not effective. The Black preacher who effectively combines imagination with role playing and spontaneous dramatization can hardly fail to reach, hold, and lift the Black audience.

Related to role playing is the common and very creative custom of using the best folk storytelling techniques (as mentioned in chap. 4). Characters are often elaborately developed. The details used give the audience many ways to identify with and learn from the experience of the character in the story. The following story from a sermon by S. M. Lockridge is a good illustration of this type of detail and congregational identification:

As they went up to the temple to pray, a certain man—don't know this man's name, but the next few words tell us somewhat of his condition—a certain man that was lame from his mother's womb. When it said "lame man," that made me feel sorry for him, because it is a pitiful thing when a man has been useful and now has lost usefulness. He has become lame and not able to get around.

But when I got to thinking about this man who was lame, and I remember the writer said that he was lame from his mother's womb, that made it all the more pitiful to me. For not only was he a lame man, but he had been lame all his life. And I can't think of nothing more pitiful than a lame baby—one who was born into the world and whose parents have ever hoped some day he will be strong and healthy. I can see those parents watching him day in and day out, but he never had any use of his limbs. He grew old in age, but still lame.

I think it was last fall, or some time recently, a teenager was told that one of his legs would have to be amputated. He just hated the idea. "Here I am a teenager, where all of the other children my age are active in getting around, doing this and that; and conditions are such that I will have to lose one of my legs and be a cripple the rest of my life." You remember he tried to run away from home because he didn't want his leg amputated.

Well, it is a pitiful thing to see a teenager lame. But, here, this man had never been able to use his limbs, and had been lame from his mother's womb. This man had to be carried. You know, we can understand this man's condition. . . . I know a lot of people in the church that are healthy and strong, but they still want to be carried. . . . They had to carry this man and they brought him daily and laid him at a gate called Beautiful. Now they carried him daily, it means that he must have been receiving something that kept him coming back. . . . Look at that man that was made by the hands of God. That man is lame and twisted, and had to be carried.

Well, when he saw Peter and John going into the temple, he got glad because, you know, he had begged so long until he could just look at a person as he approached and he could tell what kind of gift he was going to get. I can understand, somehow, how he felt. At one time I used to hop bells at a hotel. And, you know, after a few years I could look at a guest when he pulled up in front of the door, and I could pretty well tell what kind of a tip I was going to get. Oh, I could look at his bags. . . . I could look at the way he was dressed, and I could tell the type, the size of tip I was going to get.

Well, this man had been in the business so long until he could look and size up the kind of gift he was going to get. But this time he underestimated. Yes, he did! He knew that he could get a good gift from Peter and John, but he was looking for alms. He was looking for something that he could exchange at the supermarket. Oh, but Peter and John said, "Look on us." And every one of us who is the representative of the Lord ought to be able to tell the world to "look on us."[4]

The speaker then went on to make the point, finally, that the man was healed in the name and by the power of Jesus.

The Bible abounds in characters about whom such details can be developed for easy identification. In another sermon, Lockridge tells the story of poor man Lazarus, adding substantial details to enable the congregation to identify with him. In his rendition of the Lazarus story, the conflict is heightened ingeniously between what might be identified as the good guys and the bad guys, and suspense is built right up to the last moment, when there is, of course, the victory of the good guys. Another preacher I have heard led the congregation from locked door to locked door in a jail, as an angel delivered Paul. Before this the preacher had spelled out the lack of cash for a bail bondsman for Paul, a very familiar story to the people who live in the Black ghettos and who often find themselves held in the White man's jail on equally questionable charges.

While these stories are highly entertaining, they are also very effective Black preaching. For the Black preacher, the victory of the good guys is not a cheap, contrived thing. Underneath it all is the clear implication of the final victory of God, of justice and righteousness. For disinherited people, no doctrine is more essential to survival and to the ability to remain creative in one's struggle for liberation.

For the purposes of Black preaching, the conflict is not between good cops and bad robbers, nor is it between heroic Western law men and outlaw cowboys. In fact, it is not a morality play related to any typical middle-class model of virtue. It is the conflict of the powerless with the powerful, the have-nots against the haves. To frame it as the just against the unjust is perhaps the closest possible way to correlate the Black conflict with the society which oppresses. As always, the conflict in the narrative has to be that which is personally crucial to the hearer.

The Use of Subjectivity and Rhetorical Flair

This whole matter of personal involvement also affects the style of the preacher from within. The inner fervor of a preacher has great importance. In Black culture it does not hurt to be one's own best customer, moved by one's own utterance. To be sure, it may seem crude to flaunt, "I'm beginning to feel pretty good now." But the self-contained, conversational tone of some preachers cannot be maintained by the Black preacher, who is expected to be caught up in sharing the Word. Black preachers have to let go. They feel what they are preaching about: freedom, sorrow, fear, rage, and joy. They must make no pretense of so-called objectivity. You can't be objective when God lays hands on you. You "preach what the Spirit say preach, and you do what the Spirit say do!"

This love of subjectivity notwithstanding, the Black congregation responds to beauty of language—to the well-turned phrase. This does not mean complexity of structure. In fact, Black-culture preachers often use short, easily remembered sentences. But they use rhetorical flair. And the Black deacon also loves to pray in highly poetic language. The flow and phraseology of the King James Version will never die in America while Black Christianity stays Black.

This flourish can be taken too far, of course. There are still some preachers of all groups who are brazenly ornate. They pay the price for their linguistic acrobatics by diverting attention from the focus of the sermon (if there be any) to themselves. In fact it is probable that the present academic inclination to use dour, barren language, offered in the name of simplicity, is a direct reaction to the flowery excesses of many preachers of a past generation. On the other hand, for Blacks and for many others capable of spiritual warmth, the impact of the lessons of the faith is greatly enhanced by the natural poetry and music of gifted preachers. Gardner C. Taylor is a case in point. Real soul preaching demands rhetorical flair. This is not to imply that good Black preaching uses rhetoric for a crutch. In fact, in my study of Black sermons, raw rhetoric was absent from the celebrative utterance more often than not. Perhaps it would be accurate to say that one of the many strengths of good Black preaching is the skillful use of poetic rhetoric.

The Use of Slow Delivery

Another characteristic of most Black preaching is a slow rate of delivery. Statistics for a scientific comparison with other groups do not exist, as far as I know. One difficulty is that the selection of a valid Black sample is complicated by the fact that there are, here and there, accomplished Black preachers with a truly rapid-fire delivery. On the whole, however, it seems unquestionable that most successful Black preaching uses a significantly lower-than-average number of words a minute. Black preachers take their time. When they are preaching, there is nothing more important that anybody there could be doing or listening to.

This attitude has some interesting implications. One might logically expect the content of the Black sermon to be scant. Not so.

The deliberate rate of the Black preacher can be more than compensated for by the increase in the length of the sermon. Another misconception might be that the preachers have to go slow because they cannot go fast. Wrong again. The Black preacher measures the delivery to increase comprehension and influence as much as possible. Many Black preachers could radically increase the rate without violence to the quality of delivery if circumstances demanded.

The fundamental significance of the slow rate is impact on the whole person: on cognitive, intuitive, and emotive consciousness. The intelligent preacher knows that true comprehension is holistic. No matter how quick the mind, the Black hearer needs time for the essence to sink into all sectors of the psyche. No human mind operates by pushing buttons and with lightning speed. So the Black preacher slows the rate and deals deliberately with the material, to the end that the congregation never has the sense of being rushed.

The Black slave song or Negro spiritual is an interesting parallel to the slow rate characteristic of the Black preaching style. The Black-culture sermon is the homiletical twin to the spiritual. In the case of the latter, a whole song can be formed on a base of very few words. Haunting choruses are built on as few as four words: "Remember me, O Lord, remember me." Whereas hymns of other cultures have long stanzas full of words delivered at a fairly rapid rate, a Black spiritual might simply say slowly, "Lord, I want to be a Christian in my heart." The slow rate of Black preaching, as well as repetition, is the natural pattern of Black speaking and singing, neither of which is prone to depend on great numbers of words or abstract thought.

The Use of Aphorisms and Hesitation

There are two stylistic features of less magnitude. One is the use of aphorisms—clever, pithy statements. Although this is fairly common in preaching of all cultures, it would appear that the use of aphorisms is more frequent among the great Black preachers of America. It is also apparent that the response of the Black audience to aphorisms is much greater than is typical in other churches. In the case of two very popular speakers, revival sermons in strange churches were introduced by a series of aphorisms. The aphorisms were extraneous and unrelated to one another, but the result for both preachers was, as intended, the building of excellent rapport with the new congregation. With this warm-up, the preachers could begin the real task of the sermon, certain of the attention of the congregation.

Another feature of smaller consequence is the stammer or hesitation. In addition to building suspense and increasing interest in the message ultimately to be delivered, this technique portrays the preacher as one who seems to be groping for the truth, struggling to hear what is coming from above. This is not altogether limited to Black preaching. It does have, however, greater currency in the ghetto, where it has the additional effect of discouraging an impression of overwhelming intellect and slick presentation. It gives an image of weakness with which the mostly underdog congregation can sympathize and identify. As the preacher searches and gropes, the members of the congregation cry, "Help him, Lord!" as evidence of their warm identification with the speaker.

*   *   *

Clearly, all of these stylistic features have more to commend them than simple habit. The subtle implications of every single feature or mannerism are consciously or unconsciously weighed before that feature becomes a permanent part of the good Black preacher's style. This is true whether the preacher is formally educated or is without any schooling. The most I can establish from comparative studies is some evidence that formal education increases the range of features used by the preacher. Conversely, every feature used by a speaker not formally trained I found to be duplicated by one or another speaker with formal training. In other words, the styles of learned and unlearned preachers completely overlap, indicating a rather strong, independent strain of preaching technique indigenous to Black culture.

A Louisiana-born minister with a bachelor of divinity degree from a recognized Midwestern graduate school of theology was once asked what effect his theological training had had on his preaching. This minister, the son of a minister and well immersed in Black religious culture long before he went to seminary, said "None!" This may not be strictly true in one sense, but the fact is that the man in question represents many Black preachers who have strength and impact in the pulpit precisely because they keep the features they learn at home and reject many of the alien notions about preaching promoted by the seminary. This great sin of the seminaries in earlier years is now being corrected in many places. Meanwhile, Black preachers must certainly maintain identity and remain Black in style, thus keeping the ability subtly to relate to their congregations in all the ways possible.

CHAPTER 7

The Black Context
for Preaching

Of great significance to the character of Black preaching is the setting in which Black preaching takes place. The Black style, which includes the call and response, is part of a larger dialogical pattern traceable to West African culture. The response requires a participating audience, and Black preaching has had such an audience from its beginning.

Black preaching has been shaped by interaction with the listeners. If the Black preaching tradition is unique at all, then that uniqueness depends significantly upon the uniqueness of the Black congregation, which talks back to the preacher as a normal part of the pattern of worship. By many outside the culture, the dialogue between preacher and congregation has been viewed, at best, as a quaint overreaction of simple folk, as exuberant expression of a beautiful, childlike faith such as could never occur in sophisticated Christian worship. At worst, this dialogue has been judged as the monkeyshines of a religious revelry, or a game run by preachers. At times, congregations have undoubtedly been manipulated by the preacher. At other times, congregations have voluntarily overparticipated as a catalyst for ecstasy—a means of escaping the pain of living in this kind of world. Yet few preachers of any race can deny that their own powers are enhanced in the spiritual dialogue that takes place with the authentic Black congregation. Most preachers of any culture would gladly welcome such stimulation and support every Sunday, if it were to be offered by their congregations. In fact, the general decline of the preaching event (apart from that of the media) could well be arrested by a transfusion of this sort.

In the participatory response of their congregations, Black preachers have a rare resource which requires greater understanding and appreciation. This might well begin with a careful description, followed by such questions as: What is Black dialogue besides a cultural habit? How does it help preachers from both inside and outside Black culture? In what understandable ways does God use this originally African phenomenon to his glory and the uplift of persons in Black America?

Black Dialogue: A Description

Black dialogue between congregation and preacher consists of the well-known cries "Amen!" "Praise the Lord!" "Well!" "Have mercy!" "Sho 'nough!" and a hundred other spontaneous audible responses. It also includes facial expressions, swaying bodies, nodding heads, raised hands, foot patting, shouting, tears, and (in recent years) hand clapping. Whatever the form, the communication is real.

It may even include coaching. When some folks feel it's time to celebrate they may without hesitation cry, "Come on up!" If it appears that a preacher's strength is waning, one may cry "Help him, Lord." When a point is especially new or needed, one may hear, "Stay right there!" And one may even hear "Hush!" when the ecstasy is too great to bear. And the coaching may go both ways, since some preachers are not willing to leave response up to the Holy Spirit. They may make a variety of candid appeals for support: "Are you praying with me?" "You're getting mighty quiet out there." "Can I get a witness?" "Amen, lights!" (since the people aren't saying anything).

A moving set of signals is to be seen in certain key words. If a preacher says that the women came to the tomb early in the morning, a pause should be left for the echo of the word *early*. Indeed, there will be disappointment and even criticism if the preacher fails to let the hearers have their part. The words *truly* and *surely* have the same value and role. If one quotes the 23rd Psalm in the celebration, saying "Surely goodness and mercy shall follow me all the days of my life," one does well to leave a pause after "Surely."

On the other hand, a preacher who preaches too long may be advised to "Come on in!" Or dead silence may be another signal that the nourishment of the Word has already ceased. Whatever the response, positive or negative, the Black worshiper of the majority of congregations feels authorized to express himself or herself freely, and this expression is used of God to provide meaningful participation in the preaching event.

Although the dialogue in which we are primarily interested is the authentic or sincere participation of persons in response to the preached Word, it is necessary to differentiate between authentic dialogue and the various species of unauthentic response. While it is much easier to name it than to do it, the very existence of unauthentic response is what has caused authentic dialogue to be overlooked or underestimated.

My studies of preaching tapes and my observations of live preaching reveal a strong correlation between real dialogue and the spiritual depth at which the sermon is pitched. This sincere response is to be distinguished from habitual (perfunctory) or manipulative dialogue. There is a difference between an Amen from the heart, which registers the considered approval of the worshiper, and the automatic, nonthinking response, which may punctuate the sermon, no matter what the preacher says. The nonthinking responder is simply reacting without hearing, assuming a customary role in the worship without bothering to know what has been said. At other times, such a person wants the preacher to sound impressive and therefore is rooting for the preacher as a kind of one-person cheering squad, no matter what is said. These patterns of insincerity sound almost demonic, but they seem less evil when one faces the fact that this is the responders' only place in life to be seen and heard, and the sermon is, actually, extremely important in their world.

Real dialogue, on the other hand, is more easily discernible. It occurs characteristically in response to the preacher's mention of something that is vital in the life experience of the respondent—something with which the hearer identifies deeply. The congregants are able to respond because they are at ease. They are interested in what the preacher is saying, because they are crucially involved in the issues considered, and deeply interested in the Bible, from which the sermon comes.

The Familiar in Dialogue

The best Black dialogues between preacher and congregation that I have studied have been uniformly prone to start with familiar biblical and living materials, which stretch the thinking and increase the insights of the hearers. The familiar is used as a model for understanding the unfamiliar. Minds and spirits are propelled into the unknown along trajectories established by association with previous experiences. At times these dialogues included parables, even as did Jesus. At other times they simply included such colorful descriptions that ancient biblical experiences were entered into vicariously and bridged over into modern life. Hearers engaged in self-recognition and thus received some firm word about God's love and will for them.

The term "hermeneutic" is most fittingly applied to this process of spiritual growth. A preacher who does not have this capability flirts with boredom and loss of attention. Black worshipers want to be stirred; they want to have an emotional experience. But they also want to be stretched, helped, and fed. They want the cream of the Black pulpit—the kind of preaching that is highly relevant in content and charismatic in delivery. When such content and imaginative delivery grips a congregation, the ensuing dialogue between preacher and people is the epitome of creative worship. Group participation works to increase impact and retention. The strength of the Black tradition at its best is the ability to combine fresh insight with impact—to feed the people and yet to keep them sensitive to the Spirit of God, which is always moving, always dynamic. Good dialogue is never static, weak, or apologetic. It is the grateful result of the hearer's fresh ownership of a Word from the Lord.

The process of spiritual illumination is illustrated in an unpublished sermon preached by Vernon Johns (1892–1965), former professor at Lynchburg College and Seminary and predecessor of Martin Luther King, Jr., at the Dexter Avenue Baptist Church in Montgomery. The sermon, titled "On Human Destiny," was preached at a session of the Hampton University Ministers' Conference. The sermon stimulated enthusiastic response, even though the growth it required might have seemed too demanding:

Now, you know, your definition of home enlarges as you travel. If a man asked me in Baltimore, "Where do you live?" I would say, "1134 McCullouh Street." If he asked me in New York, "Where do you live?" I would say, "In Baltimore." If he asked me in Canada, "Where do you live?" I would say, "The United States of America." And if he asked me in Europe, "Where do you live?" I would say, "In America." You see, your definition of home enlarges as you move out. [Great response.] And if my little grandchild heard that I was dead, and asked what happened to Granddad, I would like for my daughter to say, "That which drew from out of the boundless deep turned again home." [Tremendous response.] And, you know, as I get older, instead of thinking of Farmville as my home, I like to say, as someone has said, . . . "I like to think of God who is our Home." [Great response.][1]

As has been noted, worship among Whites and Blacks was similar during the Great Awakenings. It might now be asked why audible response or dialogue disappeared from mainline Protestant patterns of worship. One guess is that the preaching material soared beyond the intellectual reach of the congregation. This occurred, perhaps, because Protestant seminaries had engaged in a contest of one-upmanship with the graduate divisions of the liberal arts colleges, creating scholars instead of professionals skilled in reaching people. With such standard conditioning in the theological schools, the preacher might well be expected to be intellectual in concerns rather than interested in the day-to-day issues of ordinary people. It follows that in such a school-conditioned, abstract atmosphere, answering back would soon be considered by the preaching scholar as impolite and disruptive. This attitude would increase the inhibitions of an audience eager to please. Modern-day experiments in the middle-class church, in which dialogue takes place during and after the sermon, seem clearly to support this hypothesis. In the planning of the talk-back after service, great care is taken to pitch the dialogue within intellectual reach of the laity involved. It is encouraging to speculate that the middle-class model may now be drifting away from the graduate classroom and back to the pattern once shared by Blacks and Whites in the preaching event.

Black response is built on this model of participation within grasp. It happens to square with the best educational concepts, both in starting where people are and in keeping them directly involved in the sermon, as God's Word unfolds. The hearers' gratitude for growth reinforces their gains in spiritual development.

Dialogue and Felt Need

Equal in importance to the concept of intellectual grasp is the concept of felt need, as an element of call-and-response. To be sure, scholarly problems are important. Ontology and epistemology must be considered by someone. But how can one engage in dialogue with the preacher in depth when one has not so much as heard if there be such a thing as ontology? Black preaching at its best has remained focused on problems that people confront daily and feel real needs in meeting. People who are oppressed are often preoccupied with problems. The Black preacher has had to give strength for the current day's journey, the guidance and vision for extended survival in an absurdly trying existence.

One of the graces of the Black ancestors was that they were beset with no temptation to begin their sermons in books in the first place. They had few books. There was little alternative to a here-and-now orientation. How a learned clergyperson might have styled an address or sermon on the problem of evil would be quite different in the hands of a Black preacher. If one dared to phrase the sermon as a question, such as "Does God Care?" or "Is God Just?" or "Can God Deliver?" then it would obviously have to be rhetorical. What the Black audience requires for the dialogue is both gut-survival themes and nourishing certainty. This is what they live by. They seem to say, "Be as learned as you like. Indeed, we want a smart preacher! But talk about something we can enter into, and give us something practical and certain."

An example of how the theme of the care of God can be illuminated with modern knowledge, while maintaining both the Black dialogue and the idiom, and offering solid certainty, is found in these excerpts from a sermon on the subject of fate:

God gets blamed for an awful lot of things that he never willed should happen. We feel we have said something that makes God look good . . . never realizing how badly we have misrepresented him when we are through. . . . Every now and then I feel I ought to tell a Brother, "This is what you are doing with these coffin nails [cigarettes]." In response, the Brother all too frequently says, "Well, you know we're not going to die before our time." What he means is that he is going to live until God cuts him down. It never dawns on him that this is a sweeping doctrinal statement. . . . Sure, we do not have the final say on how long we shall live. But it's quite another thing to say you haven't anything at all to do with it. You see, you can speed up your death date on your own. You can do all sorts of things God never intended, and not be able to get back here next Sunday. [Great response.] . . .

Recently, after a funeral, I heard several people publicly state, "God took him. He loved him more than we did." Of course God loved him more than we. . . . His love is perfect. . . . But what they were saying is that God sent that Brother a heart attack. . . . This appears to me to be highly unlikely and downright repulsive. . . . God may be said to have given him a weaker heart than some at birth. He may have been born of parents with weaker hearts. . . . But I know some other things in this particular case. He worked around the clock. He had no rest. He was beset with . . . worry. . . . Now I'm sure that the three insurance men in this church would charge you a lot less if everybody waited until God sent for him. . . . Our lives are all too often shortened by things we have done. [Response.]. . . .

One of the texts, Genesis 1:28, says: "Subdue the earth." We are inclined to say that God is the one who controls cancer, but don't you know that even cancer is here for us to subdue! . . . If we were to put as much effort into subduing cancer as we have put into trying to subdue the Viet Cong, don't you know we'd have a cure for cancer! [Great response.] God is blamed for something he left in our own hands . . . He's waiting for us to give it everything we've got, and he will help us as needed. [Response.]. . . .

I hate to trespass on people's feelings, but I hear people asking me, "Reverend, when were you born? What month? Oh that explains it." Let me tell you, that don't explain nothin'! [Great response.] All this horoscope foolishness! God doesn't hold me responsible for my decisions and then have me born under a sign so I can't help myself. You know better than that! [Great response.]   —Henry H. Mitchell

The dialogue is lively when needs are met and the concepts used are within reach of the hearers.

Dialogue and Social Distance

In the Black preaching enterprise, the preacher's preparation starts with close identity with the congregation. Historically, as a Black, one could not escape having a part in their condition even if one wanted to. Whether chosen from the ranks of the membership (as often occurred) or not, the preacher was allowed no social distance from the people. And this is still an essential part of the Black understanding. When today's Black ghetto preacher seems removed owing to living standards, one can be sure that this is being countered by a traditional statement of need called "poor mouth," and by making "Aunt Jane" and all the rest aware that the preacher needs their help and support desperately, while struggling with the load. The Black preacher must be ear deep in the condition of the people, and out of this comes the easy dialogue between the preacher and the people, whose lives are intimately close together—so close together that the themes which invade the consciousness of the one also invade the other.

This intimacy leads people to feel literally that they are being addressed personally. Most Black preachers, if they have held a pastorate for any length of time, have been unjustly accused on occasion of meddling and revealing confidences, because the sermon material used was so close to home for one or another member. Even when hearers are most grateful for a helpful message, they have been known to ask if a relative talked with the preacher the week preceding and revealed what was happening. On the whole, closeness has been a very positive value, interpreted in love and prone to reflect the close, warm relatedness of the true Christian community. In a sense, Black audiences find it difficult not to talk back to a person so close to them. The habit of personal response to preaching persists and has become a part of the culture generally.

Dialogue influences relations between pulpit and pew even when the preacher is completely unfamiliar and not a close personal figure at all. Or perhaps better said, the feeling of closeness to the messenger carries through to all preachers among those who have habitually engaged in meaningful Black dialogue. A preacher may even hear a response to meaningless material. This leads to the clear and undeniable implication that some Black dialogue is conditioned in some sense, as previously discussed. In theory, a preacher could intone, "Corn bread and collard greens is mighty good eatin'," and someone might respond with a fervent "Amen!" It is a well-known fact that some Black preachers are very adept at the use of the right cliches and the right tone to elicit audible response. But this is not the whole story. Not by any means.

No preacher can accurately predict what the reception will be or what God will accomplish through his or her efforts. The important issue here is that how the hearers respond will always have at least something to do with how close to or how far from the preacher they feel personally. With the best of rapport, the majority of Black preachers would assume that God must still help them, both directly and through the congregation's participation in the dialogue, if an in-depth spiritual happening is to occur. Meanwhile, there is a blessed unpredictability that keeps Black preachers at least a little humble and keeps their audiences in a state of expectancy, always wondering which way the truth will unfold and which direction the winds of the Spirit will blow. This inability to encounter the gospel using a formula is applauded by all. Humble pastors prefer minimal social distance and enjoy the fact that the dialogic response and eternal results are in God's hands.

Dialogue and Activism

There is, however, a serious question in the minds of some Black preachers regarding the ultimate impact of dialogue, not that they object to this Black oral tradition, but for fear the joys of it take the edge off social activism. Vernon Johns, who was an advocate of Black culture and Black pride, had the following to say to a large audience of Black preachers at Hampton University:

I really believe that in our religion so much noise is, in actuality, a substitute for action. [Loud response, laughter.] You know, when a man is impressed with something, he feels he just ought to do something about it. So what he decides to do is holler about it. [Laughter, cheers.] Let me tell you, that's a lot cheaper than acting—a whole lot cheaper. [Widespread responses like "Whooee!"][2]

Dr. Johns was equally critical of cold, unresponsive worship, however, and he himself extolled the lively audience more than once. What he says is not designed to eliminate dialogue, but seeks to discipline and focus it toward empowerment. His brilliant successor at the Dexter Avenue Church, Martin Luther King, Jr., was modern America's greatest activist preacher, not in spite of his warm dialogue with the Black masses, but because of it. The "I Have a Dream" address was in fact a sermon, which drew dialogue from thousands and moved the Civil Rights cause forward by giant steps on many fronts.

Dialogue has also put Black hearers "on the record" for their Christian faith and practice, and for the cause they have affirmed. There is a sense in which one has greater ownership of and identification with the gospel when one has also been privileged to make one's own witness right there in the worship. Dialogue, then, is not just quietistic pietism; it strengthens and motivates the labors of those who engage in unashamed response to a powerful Word from the Lord.

Order in Spontaneity

The very concept of discipline and focus may seem to be foreign to Black spontaneity. Certainly, some limits need consideration. For example, concern is often expressed for some semblance of liturgical order. The Black middle-class mind, relatively less involved in the culture of the Black masses, is prone to fear the potential chaos (a stronger word for unpredictability) resulting from the dynamics of the in-depth encounter found in Black-culture worship. There is also the danger that the experience-centered worship will become an end in itself, devoid of reasonable elements of enlightenment or spiritual worth.

Such concerns appear smaller on the Black agenda than perhaps they should. Many sensitive, intelligent Blacks who are deeply committed to Black identity and culture have left the Black-culture church because they did not see enough discipline and positive direction to justify the huge investment of resources consumed by the Black church. However Spirit-led the spontaneity may be, losses like this cannot be written off or blamed on a God whose will it is not to lose any.

Another concern for discipline deals with time. There is valid reason to ask why the worship service in Black churches should last so long. Modern Black youth are turned off by services lasting two-and-a-half to three hours. Many of these youth leave, and others refuse to come to church at all. Black adults of thoughtful dedication would welcome the careful stewardship of time spent in service. Yet Black tradition holds that the Holy Spirit does not follow man-made clocks. There ought to be some sacred time in a life of oppression when the clock is not lord. The Spirit must have its way, and whatever God does is right on time. It is believed that the true Presence is intellectually as well as emotionally enlightening, and that the Spirit needs time to involve a congregation deeply in the counter-culture of worship.

When all of this is granted, the concern for time involves more than the worldly, business-like restriction of worship to sixty minutes. Today's Blacks are not interested in wasting time any more than Whites are. However long or short the service is, they prefer not to be bored with uninteresting, irrelevant announcements and presentations, and sermons full of useless redundancy or scattered ad libs. Black worship, in many places, still needs better planning before and after the main fare of the sermon. To do this will not hamper the Spirit one iota. Punctually begun and with sensitive preparation, a truly Black service need not require more than one-and-a-half to two hours, with all the participation one could wish for. All too often, longer services reflect not the activity of God but the laxity of people and the ambitious, endless repetitions of singing groups.

On the other hand, stripping down to two hours may still exceed the attention span of some Christians. In their willingness to spend two full hours meaningfully, Black congregations still evidence two differences from those who prefer to spend less time in worship. One difference is that Black worship is not watched but participated in, in depth. However much Black worship appears to the outsider to be a spectator activity, it is in fact a gripping involvement with relatively little chance for the participants to worry about passage of time. Pastors who insist on lengthy anticlimactic ad libs are chastened by the fact that people leave when the service loses its grip. The other difference is that the worshiper is considered worthy to participate, thus adding to the reward or satisfaction. Underneath the most rigid middle-class commitments to keep faith with people, respect their calendars, and let "busy folks" out on time (in one hour) is a relegation of these supposedly important people to a do-nothing spectator role so that the bases can all be touched in a hurry.

One of the Black spirituals hints that people "keep so busy praisin' Jesus they ain't got time to die." The time spent in worship is not forced; it is enjoyed. It is an avenue of highly satisfying self-expression. Who needs to go home? Perhaps more important on the Black agenda is this: What could possibly take preeminence over this duty to God, which is at the same time so enjoyable to the worshiper?

Dialogue and Contagion

Another aspect of the congregational setting of Black preaching is its contagion. The joy of those most committed has always influenced the response and the satisfaction of the entire congregation. Black preachers have come to depend very heavily on a small cadre of souls, long in prayer and receptive to the Spirit, to set the tone of the preaching dialogue.

The possibility conceded that some few may respond fervently just by habit or to trigger a general response for the preacher, the more serious worshipers may take on several much more positive roles. Some people cheer the athlete (or the preacher) more readily when others are already cheering. The early responders have already been primed by prayer and are themselves deeply involved in this Black worship experience. They often have little understanding of the deeper significance and contagious impact of their very presence and verbal response.

Another very positive role of the worshiper is implied by all that has been said about dialogue; it is the role of stimulator or initiator of the dialogue. Somebody has to be ready to participate when the sermon begins. If Black preaching is in fact dialogue, then it must be dialogue, at least, to some extent, from the very beginning of the sermon. A dull, uncommunicative start may establish a pattern or a relationship between preacher and congregation that cannot subsequently be changed. There simply is no dialogue when only one person is speaking.

This suggests still another role of the worshiper, that of showing close rapport with the speaker. As has been noted, Black dialogue involves a kind of intimacy of feeling. Such rapport is not achieved instantaneously by everyone. If there are some whose rapport with God through prayer has made them more open to immediate communication in depth with the preacher, then this helps others to achieve a similar rapport. It says to the hesitant and the uncertain that it is safe or acceptable to open up to the Spirit, who is present through the preaching of the Word. Even if the responsive readiness of some is based on less lofty reasons than prayer, an influence on the larger group may still take place, and all of this may be to the glory of God and the improvement of the gospel event.

There is another sense in which the opening up of the worshiper to the preacher is only a part of a larger opening up to God and the group as a whole. Modern therapy and sensitivity training have shown the value of self-revelation in a safe environment. The risk of self-disclosure is not readily acceptable to many Blacks. They have had to be close-lipped and poker-faced to survive. Because they have been of necessity such great actors and self-concealers, they do not readily respond to any therapeutic formula requiring self-disclosure. And yet there must be some place where Blacks can actually open up and express their feelings safely. The Black church has been that place.

The healing catharsis inherent in the permissive, person-affirming Black worship service has enabled many generations of Blacks to keep their balance and sanity in a world where other racial groups with far fewer problems have chosen suicide. Statistically speaking, suicide was, until recently, a disease of the American White male. The beleaguered Blacks had a balm that others did not know about.

Their belief system and worship tradition gave them a motive for "keeping on keeping on," regardless of circumstances. No matter what the external stresses, the church was a safe haven of love and free expression. It was and is a blessed tradition.

The Black congregation is one of the most dynamic and healing of places known to humanity. There may be tares with the wheat, but they who leave the field because of a few tares may starve to death in the midst of bounteous plenty. With all of its flaws, Black dialogic worship is one of the best ways anywhere to hear and be healed.

Dialogue as Resource

From a preacher's point of view, the Black congregation with its contagious response is the best group in the world to whom to preach the gospel. The dialogue is freeing and affirming to the preacher. Not only is it easier to preach in the midst of authentic dialogue; but also the quality of preaching increases. Here and there one may encounter overreaction or virtual dominance of a service, but this is rare. I can remember no more than two complaints about congregational response in my more than fifty years of preaching the gospel. Congregational response is so important that without it, there could be no genuinely Black sermon. Sandy F. Ray (1898–1979), the late pastor of the Cornerstone Baptist Church of Brooklyn, casually and comically stated the case in unforgettable words:

He [a friendly White Southern Baptist minister] said to me, "Sandy, I know you can preach. You can preach *any*where, and we want to hear you preach like you preach in *your* church."
I said, "I don't think I can do that."
"Don't you bother about us. You just preach the gospel."
"That's just like asking a doctor to perform a major operation, when he only has his bag with him. If he's going to perform a major operation, he has to have all of his equipment. He has to be in a hospital where he has all the nurses, all the other attending doctors, and an operating room. You can't have a major operation just with a bag. If you want me to preach like I preach at home, you have to have somebody to say at the proper place, 'Come on up!'"
They were very nice to me *after* I preached. But when I played baseball, I wanted the people to cheer me when I was playing. I didn't need them after the game was over.[3]

112

Thousands of Black preachers would heartily agree with me in concurring with this appraisal of the importance of dialogue in the Black tradition. The richness of the Black pulpit tradition is inextricably bound up with this oft overlooked resource, the congregation, without whom the sermon event would be impossible.

CHAPTER 8

The Black Sermon

In keeping with the Black affirmation of personal styles, imagination, and spontaneity, it is impossible to establish a single definitive outline for a Black sermon. We could cite as fairly typical, illustration, storytelling, Black language and style, and Black celebration. The routes by which the sermon arrives at the celebrative conclusion, however, are as many and varied as the preachers themselves, the various audiences, and the dialogues between them occurring in each of the sermons. So we cannot engage here in an exhaustive discussion of overall structure.

Generally speaking, Black preaching is probably as varied in structure as White preaching, except that more Black sermons are apt to consist of one single Bible narrative (with or without extended comments on the side). Thus the percentage of classical or traditional sermons—with text, exposition, the inevitable trinity of points or applications, and climax—would be somewhat lower in the Black total. In addition, Black preaching, even when there are such "points," tends not to sound so carefully organized. The force of the message does not hinge so much on logical persuasion of the sort in which the preacher scores points in an essay or a debate. Thus, when Black preachers are most persuasive, they are apt to seem more to plead out of passion than to argue out of logic. They seek to guide the hearers in an experience, rather than to overwhelm them with intellectual evidence, even though they may use it well. And they would probably have no formal term to describe what they do.

My own observations seem to show no correlation between a high response or effectiveness and any one type of structure. The variations in response seem much more related to personal charisma. It would be safe to say that White preachers use no approach to sermon organization that might not also be very effective, in the hands of a given Black preacher, with a Black congregation. It would obviously be equally true that no approach, no matter how typical of Black preaching, can guarantee effectiveness if the preacher does not have the gift to use it with charisma or power. A great deal of what gives Black preaching this power is not to be captured in writing.

The elements of a Black sermon are not unique, and we shall deal with them in sequence. The purpose of dealing with these elements at all will be to point out, within the typical categories, the various ways in which Black sermons tend to "do it differently."

Introductions

Introductions are of two types: the self-introduction of the preacher to a new audience, and the introduction of the sermon itself. In the case of the self-introduction, Black preaching demands an intimate relationship between preacher and people which cannot be expected just to happen. It is not hard for a new voice to be heard, especially if cordially introduced, but speakers are obligated to put their own finishing touches on the necessary rapport. It is also true that speakers have the need to establish their own feelings of intimacy and confidence in a new setting. Guest preachers in the Black pulpit are permitted to ad lib for a while, until they have achieved a bond with the congregation.

Guest preachers among the masses are also required to give due respect to God and to all of the real and imaginary dignitaries on the platform. One never invades the sacred pulpit of another without proper recognition and thanks for the honor. Greater love hath no preacher than this, that he or she give up the pulpit for a brief season. One mentions other preachers, church officers, and dear friends, all because these "praise speeches" are as old as the West African culture from which they came. Whereas I once resented this as a waste of time, I have come to see the profound value of such honor. It is valuable for reasons of cultural momentum, and because there is so little honor paid the oppressed in any other arena.

In the introduction of the message itself, the approach tends also to be very personal. That is, an effort is made to establish some issue or

115

entity with which the hearers identify immediately. Rather than logically starting with a broad category and narrowing the focus, the best Black sermons start with an important issue, and the listeners get on board the experience. The sermon near the end of chapter 2 was reported by a layperson seventy years later with amazing accuracy because this person had been drawn "on board." When the preacher, Uncle Pompey, took his text where Paul and Silas were in jail, the vital relevance to the death of a man who had been sentenced to jail was established. Not a soul would have dared stop listening from there on.

The issue of humor in introductions is often raised in classes on Black preaching. The positive side is that humor can do much to help both speaker and audience relax and open up to each other. But humor must be in the best of taste and held to a minimum. The telling of jokes is subject to serious question, and only the most chaste and purposeful jokes are likely to be accepted, even though the Black audience is traditionally permissive. This need for humor to be relevant applies throughout the sermon.

There is also the no-introduction introduction. In many Black churches the pastor is so well known and respected that the sermons tend to start instantly. A text is announced, and the sermon starts immediately, without any "form or fashion." The congregation has been trained to hunger and thirst for biblical wisdom, and they need no attention-getting opening lines. Another no-introduction situation occurs when the preacher plans to tell a story to a congregation known to love narratives. The introduction can be as dull as "Once upon a time," so long as a good narrative is sure to follow. Visitors may not have such an open receptivity, but they often take their cues from the majority of the members, acquiring anticipation by contagion.

Sermon Types

When speakers have won their way through the outer defenses and have drawn the hearers on board with a compelling issue, it is time for the main body of the message to begin. Good introductions will create a desire for the text out of which the sermon flows, in most cases. The introduction ends with a sentence which leads into the biblical material. It is then that the main body of the sermon normally begins.

I perceive three main types of sermons to be common in the Black pulpit: *textual* and *expositional,* to use the terms of James Earl Massey, nationally known radio preacher and teacher of preachers; and *narrative* (which Massey includes in expositional).[1] I might add a fourth type, the sermon built on a figure or *metaphor,* but this would also be included in one of Massey's two types above. This is immediately apparent in the outline below of a textual sermon, the flow of which is based on a metaphorical figure—that of footracing. Massey defines the first two types as follows:

The textual sermon has a "design determined mainly by the divisions or sequences of thought in a single text or short passage from Scripture." The Black preacher's task is to make those divisions come alive in the mind of the hearer. Thus the painting of pictures and telling of stories becomes the basis for the moves or points within the text. The structure may be relatively standard, but the way in which the text is exegeted or elaborated could include every way of lively communication known to the Black tradition.

A sermon on Hebrews 12:1-2 would likely include the following moves, which would be typical in any culture:

1) We are surrounded by a cloud (crowd) of sainted and beloved witnesses.
2) So as not to disappoint them, it would be a good idea to lay aside every weight and sin.
3) We can then run with patience this marathon race.
4) And when we look to Jesus, we are reminded of the joy at the end of the race. (celebration)

The Black preacher will be very biblical but also very vivid, and the hearers will see themselves actually warming up and stripping down and running. This is what the writer of Hebrews meant to happen, and this is the Bible communicated in the best possible manner. It may not be quite so proper and dignified as some might desire, but it will have "gut" impact and give power to the gospel. Children will listen attentively, and some menfolk will be more interested than usual. Years later, someone will say, "I can *see* that old preacher now, as he took us out on the track and got us ready for the race." And all the lessons attached to the figure will be better retained in memory and also better placed in practice.

Massey's second form is the expositional, which he defines as a design "determined basically by an extended passage of Scripture."

This is not to be confused with the verse-by-verse "expository" treatment, which gives a wide variety of sermon ideas and deals in depth with none of them. Good expositional preaching in any culture will be focused or centered on one main idea and purpose in the passage. The task of the Black preacher, again, is simply to make it come alive, as in the outline just given.

The way that the passage is to come alive will be determined, as Massey suggests, by the genre of the passage.[2] If it is a letter from Paul to the difficult church at Corinth, then the preacher will get into Paul's head and worry about what's going on in Corinth. Then, thinking out loud, the preacher will write the letter-sermon. The whole congregation will join in the experience, and engage in self-recognition, which motivates growth. The people listening will no doubt be guilty of the same things, but they will overhear the Word directed against Corinthian sin better than if they had been put on the defensive about their own. The process of overhearing has been covered well by Fred Craddock,[3] but it is also related to an old African tradition anthropologists refer to as ritual insult. It is the permission to be candid by indirection.

The fact that the Black congregation tends to enjoy the way the Bible comes alive in these two types must not be mistaken for childishness or light-hearted handling of serious concerns. The humor of self-recognition not only guarantees that the hearers visualize what the preacher said, but it also assures the preacher that they see and feel the relevance to their own lives. The Word is working in the depths, and one has only to see how people act toward the end of the sermon to know that this is no child's play.

The third form, which I have called the narrative or storytelling sermon, is deadly serious as well, no matter how entertaining it may be. Storytelling is discussed in chapter 4 (see pp. 69-72). It is mentioned again here because there are many Black sermons that are stories and nothing more. When the story begins or ends, the sermon does the same. The divisions or dramatic "acts" in the story are the moves of the sermon, which is why Massey places storytelling in his expositional type or category. There may be, however, a big difference, in the sense that the narrative sermon is a single-focus work of art. The biblical accuracy of a narrative sermon is not negotiable, but its effectiveness is dependent on an artistry that goes beyond exposition.

Just as it is true that figures or metaphors may be used in either the textual or the expositional sermon, and just as it is true that a whole sermon may be built on a single story, it is also true that a whole sermon may use a single metaphor. This one-figure sermon constitutes a fourth sermon type. The moves would simply be based on several parallels between the figure and human experience. I recall sermons on fishing—studying the fish's habits, choosing the bait to match the taste of the fish sought, waiting with patience, and pulling in the fish—which acknowledged that to be caught for Christ is life, not death. The text, of course, would be "I will make you fishers of men" (Matt. 4:19).

The advantage of figures or metaphors is not only the clarity of ideas as visualized, but also the possibility that the hearer will feel very close to the sport of fishing, for instance, and therefore become deeply involved in the message. I have given a sermon on automotive cooling systems which has delighted and deeply moved men, as well as women.[4] The moves in the sermon relate to regular maintenance (spiritual discipline), inaccurate thermostats (bad tempers), and foreign substances (selfishness) in the radiator. The very mention of the freeze plugs and gaskets and hose clamps in the holy of holies imparts a sense of sacredness to what is for some everyday labor. The Good News is that the Holy Spirit overhauls folks, as my mechanic overhauled the cooling system of our ancient car. Paul gave the text, which suggests that Christians are equipped with adequate cooling systems called longsuffering, or patience (Gal. 5:22).

This sermon includes nothing that necessarily makes it a Black sermon. The Black characteristics are in the delivery and the reception. I will always treasure the way men have come on board and quite literally have cheered the preacher on, finally coming to a time of serious dedication—a time when hands, typically too greasy ever to get clean, are folded in fervent prayer at the altar—and the way women have been overjoyed that the Word, for once, has truly reached the less pious menfolk.

Celebration

The radiator sermon closes with a celebration of the dependability of the overhauled old car and an overhauled preacher who once had a very hot temper. That celebration is the one aspect of the sermon that most nearly deserves to be called typically Black. The transcription that follows is from the end of another sermon built on a metaphor.

This time the moves were based on the various aspects of ambassadorship, to which Paul exhorts Christians in II Corinthians 5:20. One of those aspects was the fact that we do not represent ourselves. Another aspect dealt with the witness value of all that we do. The celebration began by asserting that ambassadors of Christ are automatically citizens of the Kingdom and not of this world, and it went on to celebrate the benefits of the position. In places I interrupt the excerpt from this sermon by the late Sandy F. Ray to report the response, since the impact of the sermon is almost impossible to evaluate on the basis of cold print.

I find myself enjoying it [this world] a little too much. I find myself getting along too well here—kinda getting too well adjusted. Once in a while I want something to remind me that I'm a foreigner, and a stranger, that this world is not my home.

And this will not be the end, this will not be the end. Some months ago, I was rushing home to a funeral of one of my ministers, and I was going from Columbus. In the rush I got on the wrong plane. When I got near Washington, I was asleep and the attendant came and shook me and said: "Fasten your seatbelt—we're coming into Washington." Then she said, "This flight terminates in Washington."

But I had a ticket to New York! I got terribly distressed, and as soon as we got off in Washington, I rushed up to the counter and I said, "Look, I had a New York ticket, and my flight has terminated here in Washington."

The agent said, "Oh, yes, Doctor, you go right to gate number two. *You have continuing* reservations." [Great response.]

So let me tell you, we must so work, and so serve, and so live, that when we come down to death—when death calls at the grave and says, "Your flight terminates here," there'll be another messenger who'll walk up and look at the ticket, and say, "Oh, yes, this flight does terminate, but *you have continuing reservations.*"

Then, when it comes time to go to glory—all of us gathered from the countries where we've served, all of us called in from our ambassadorial assignments—I can hear the King, as he looks over us; as he looks over our records, I want him to say: "Well done. Well done, thou good and faithful servant. You've had some rough days, and you didn't get along always too well with the foreigners, and they gave you a hard time, but you stuck it out and did a good job. Well done, well done, that's good enough!"[5] [Great response.]

Black celebration has been criticized by some for being too emotional, manipulative of people, and unnecessary to the moves of the sermon. The latter challenge is met when the celebration is relevant to the purpose of the body of the sermon. Celebration dramatizes the main idea of the sermon and supports the behavioral purpose or motivational goal. The function could be called "ecstatic reinforcement." People relate to and remember what they celebrate, and it influences their behavior.

The cardinal sin of the Black pulpit is probably that of irrelevant celebration—gravy that does not match the meat, so to speak. Good gravy is always made of the essence of the meat to be served, and the same is true of the good gospel feast. When the celebration is about something else, the real message is lost, while the celebration, if it has any substance at all, is recalled. It is vitally important that all preachers conclude by lifting up the main concerns of the sermon in genuine, joyful celebration.

The strength of these irrelevant celebrations has been that they were graphic and compelling. Stock conclusions known to slay the audience include powerful reenactments of the crucifixion, the preacher's conversion ("when the dungeon shook and the chains fell off," etc.), and scenes from the death of the preacher's mother or father. The trouble has been that they are pasted on to the end of just any old sermon, with some of the same formula words recurring Sunday after Sunday. Whatever the sermon text or purpose, the Bible is full of matching celebrations well worth searching for, and many texts, such as the Hebrews 12 text, have the celebration built right in: "for the joy that was set before him [and us]."

It is the unrelated celebration that has earned the Black pulpit the bad reputation for being manipulative. When people push the buttons for nothing more than emotive impact, the charge is well deserved. The problem is that so many Black preachers of the masses are still without formal training, and the sermons they have seen and heard all their lives have committed this same sin. A new generation of preachers with fluency in the culture and discipline in sermon preparation is beginning to change the balance by celebrating on target.

There simply must be a biblical lesson and behavioral objective that justifies stirring people's feelings. The emotional is most essential; it may not be omitted. If there is no impact in emotive consciousness, then the sermon has not influenced people where it counts most: in behaviors that are emotional, such as love and hate, fear and trust. The Black pulpit tradition is still so important because it has unshamedly addressed the whole person—the cognitive, intuitive, and emotive. People have survived still-unbelievable horrors only because their feelings of trust were regularly nourished from pulpit and fireside.

No matter how misused by some or criticized by others, the celebration at its best is the goal to which all of the Black sermon is moving. In sermon preparation, it is often the celebration that is chosen right after a text and purpose have been selected. It is on the basis of the final celebration more than any other element that the sermon will be judged. If the sermon is remembered, then it will be because the text was etched by ecstasy on the heart of the hearer.

Relevant celebration appeals to the highest emotions of hearers from any ethnic background, and the future of preaching may well depend on the recovery of the passion that once fired two Great Awakenings. America's colonies were first drawn together and united for a revolution by Whitefield's fiery preaching and the First Great Awakening, more than by any other single influence. But the emotion of this fiery preaching was well beyond the tolerance of many of the descendants of the pioneers. And the icy spirits of succeeding generations have yearned for a fresh outpouring of the Spirit, but their cultural criteria have blocked the blessings.

Today America can witness to Eastern Europe and South Africa because its commitment to freedom was increased in the 1960s by an emotional Black preacher named Martin Luther King, Jr. It can all be summed up in the scene in 1963 when King took a rhetorical flight in support of a raceless America. Thousands from every state in the nation were swept up in a crescendo of both emotional joy and hard determination. "I Have A Dream" will probably be better remembered than any sermon in all the history of these United States—not because of the intellectual soundness of this Ph.D.'s thought, nor the clever appeal to the check metaphor, but because it stirred the highest of emotions in a celebration which now belongs to the ages and to all the world.

CHAPTER 9

Toward a Theology of Black Preaching

B lack preaching is conditioned by sociology, economics, government, culture—the whole ethos of the Black community. It is also affected by (and is producing and changing) both a Black summa theologica and, in particular, a theology about itself. Much of this body of theology has been intuitive and unformulated. The process of analysis and writing has advanced greatly in the past twenty years, however. It is appropriate here to consider the theology of Black preaching. This is still only a beginning, but it is very important to state this theological basis and hope that someone will carry on.

The Sermon as Creative Partnership

The Black sermon is produced in a process which has already been established as deeply involving the congregation. Black folk-theology of the people has always gone a step farther in assuming that there is a third personal presence in the process, even the Holy Spirit. Black congregations have literally claimed the promise that "where two or three are gathered together in my name, there am I in the midst of them" (Matt. 18:20).

However stated, it has clearly been assumed that the sermon came from God. This assumption has seldom, if ever, been stated outright in terms of God as preacher, but the implication that God speaks by possessing the preacher has always been clear. In an age of secularization with an emphasis on human effort, this sounds out of step and behind the times. It is necessary, therefore, to devise a theology of preaching that properly takes into account any advances in the thinking of Christendom and still uses seriously the time-honored African and Christian language of possession.

This requires a collateral assumption about preparation that would appear to some as not typically Black. Preachers must prepare to preach. Many Black preachers seriously have held—and some still hold—that specific sermon preparation is contrary to the concept that sermons come from God. But other Black preachers (certainly those who bother to seek professional training) hold that God acts only after we have done all that we can do by way of preparation. The category "we," in this case, includes congregational preparation.

In unwitting support of the concept of the importance of human participation, many preachers, committed to the idea of God the Holy Spirit as preacher, will say when the sermon goes flat, "Somebody isn't praying!" Thus, the often unspoken assumption of Black preaching is that we bring to God our very best and ask God to take both preacher and congregation and make between them a sermon experience in which the Word and will are communicated with power.

There is no need to digress into technicalities about *how* we carry out our prior effort. Be it outline, verbatim notes, or just concentrated thought, prayer, and study about the text, during preparation there must be a serious effort to give God one's best. To do less is like asking God to do one's homework or to go to the store to buy a loaf of bread! It should be clear in any theology, Black or otherwise, that God will surely not do for us what we can do for ourselves. This is the point where secular thought has rightly criticized the tradition, and this criticism must be faced. The fact that we have the responsibility now for many things we once had to ask for in prayer must apply to every field, including preaching. What the unschooled and charismatic Black preacher once was actually given from on high (in deep and disciplined meditation) has now to be sought in part in the modern preacher's library. Then may the preacher ask of God the finishing touches. Those who ask God to do the entire task have not heard the command to subdue all things (Gen. 1:28), or to go wash in the pool of Siloam (John 9:7), or to pick up their own beds and walk (Mark 2:9, 11). In all of these God provides what is needed *after* we have done our part.

This question immediately arises: What of the spontaneity so universally accepted as Black culture's greatest trait? The riff or improvisation on the melody so characteristic of the Black jazz instrumentalist or vocalist is Black spontaneity at its best. The same freedom applied to the melodic line in Black gospels or religious soul music is the very trademark of Black culture, including the sermon. One Black intellectual, who is a popular lecturer in colleges and universities, has so embraced the concept of Black spontaneity as to make each lecture an example of spontaneity, created in dialogue with the audience on the spot. How does one relate this to the very strong declarations just made about preparation?

The answer as explained by the illustration of jazz music is clearest. No real jazz musician ever riffs on the theme until the diatonic scale, the instrument, and the theme have been mastered. When musicians do their thing, creating and playing "from the bottom of the soul," they have already practiced the basics for years. To be sure, they are creating in Black fashion, and they are in dialogue with the audience, which is comparable to the Black-preaching audience. But the least-informed Black jazz buff can feel the difference if the artist has not done the proper preparation and practice.

So it is with the Black preacher. The hearers want the Word God gives preachers on the spot. But hearers prefer that preachers be properly prepared to receive God's gift and that this preparation be done well in advance of the preaching event. God does not give by direct revelation or inspiration what the preacher can procure of God's gifts by his or her own study and discipline.

These generalities about preparation require more specific description of the format in which one brings one's personal effort to the sermon. The traditional phrasing of the issue is in terms of the old controversy between those who use a verbatim manuscript and those who use an outline, of whatever complexity or detail.

The first comment has to be that God can speak to preachers at a desk as well as in a pulpit, even with no congregation present. Therefore, although the product is a dialogue between the preacher and the congregation, the beginning may well be a dialogue between the preacher and God. This may produce either manuscripts or outlines, written or memorized. The old-school idea that only "man" speaks from a prepared paper was usually a rationalization of the unlearned preachers' disregard for books (except for the Bible) and writing. That the Bible itself was *written* by persons inspired did not seem to trouble these antiwriting people. The argument against manuscripts as quenching the Spirit is further riddled by the fact that in the Black pulpit there is never really any such thing as a verbatim manuscript. One may read every word, but the interpretation will still be different at each reading. A substantial aspect of meaning has to do with how the manuscript is read. This amounts to an impromptu reinterpretation each time a given manuscript is read, yet it is a creation which is still the product of the preacher, the congregation, and the Holy Spirit.

The prominent preachers whose tapes I have studied used manuscripts very well. But virtually all of them engaged in interludes of completely spontaneous elaborations or illustrations. On the whole, these were very plainly more effective than the passages that were read. In addition to the increased rapport with the congregation, born of the restoration of visual contact and the increased freedom and flow, there was the apparent influence of these passages as coming more from the preacher's "soul." Whether the Black manuscript preacher uses a variety of reading interpretations or lengthy, spontaneous interpolations (most use both), the fact is clear that the manuscript method of some Black preachers is used to God's own glory.

My own bias is toward a somewhat more purist approach to the spontaneity so clear in Black religious tradition. I suggest that these excellent manuscript preachers would have been still more effective if they had established their original "batting stance" in the outline tradition. On the other hand, it's not a good idea to change the batting stance of a .350 hitter, either. To return to the parallel of the improvisation on themes in jazz and gospel songs, the outline is comparable to the establishment of the theme. The outline helps the Black preacher to integrate the gift that God has already given (in the moment of illumination in the study) with what God gives directly and through the congregation when the preacher proclaims the gospel from the pulpit. In theory, at least, this outline approach seems best to provide the environment for an authentic and focused worship-happening. In fact, God gives happenings to many Black preachers in spite of their manuscripts, as well as in spite of no specific preparation. No theological theory can honestly be used to deny what so authentically comes from God.

Of course, the ultimate question is, Do even the best of Black sermons actually come from God? Again, a single statement without qualification begets reservation. A further assumption is required. Even though the Creator does speak through the medium of the

Black sermon, the process is, in fact, the product of a partnership. This partnership involves not only the preparation mentioned but also the goals and the entire message and impact. Whether it be styled to save and sanctify, to help and lift needy humankind, to praise God, or to hasten the very reign and kingdom of God, this means that the process of creating the sermon is not exclusively God's.

God, who does not *need* anything we do, has clearly left it up to us to accept the creative partnership. If one of us or all of us refuse, Black theology holds that the rocks will cry out the message (Luke 19:40). But this concept of inevitable proclamation has no literal application. It simply means that God will find a way to get the gospel preached in our time, with or without us. The verse is intended to reinforce human humility.

The creativity of the partnership between God, preacher, and hearers is vitally important. The hermeneutic principle clearly demands that preaching be more than fiery repetition of ancient shibboleths. No golden age of preaching we can look back upon was known at its inception as golden. It was too fresh and disturbing. It was recognized as golden more often only in retrospect. The Black hermeneutic, at its best, will also be very strange and new. Just as the jazz riff or the gospel-song improvisation on the melody will be a brand-new creation of the moment, so must the Black sermon be fresh and immediately relevant. It is the joint enterprise of a Creator who declares, "Behold, I make all things new" (Rev. 21:5), and a Black preacher and congregation who make themselves the instrument of innovation.

Pragmatism vs. Intellectualism

Yet newness does not imply Black uncertainty. The modern intellectual style of trying to avoid being dogmatic by being tentative (in the interest of intellectual honesty and integrity) is a luxury ill afforded in the religion of the Black ghetto. To be sure, there are intellectual areas where honesty demands open-endedness. The question is simply whether or not the Black church can afford to be concerned with such. The Black worshiper is seeking the answers to visceral questions on which life itself depends. The solution of abstract problems can wait. The important questions are more pragmatic and immediate. One will have to bet one's life on a decision tomorrow. On what shall one stake that life? "If the trumpet give an uncertain sound" (I Cor. 14:7-9), hearers will only be confused. It is to be assumed that the Black preacher has had to take the same risks. What decision did he or she make and on what grounds? If the grounds were adequate for so momentous a risk, they are adequate to be proclaimed with certainty and not cautiously offered alongside some casual ideas on which one wouldn't dream of betting a life.

There are, of course, limits to the trumpet figure. The Black preacher is not an army officer ordering men to their death. Rather, the declarer of the gospel is a crucial witness, declaring how God's children ought to live. If the preacher has no certainty about where to attack the infringements on Black personhood, how may the hearers begin to know? The Black church (and it is not alone) craves certainty, but it demands that the trumpet be informed also.

This should not be construed as meaning that open-ended questions have no place in the Black church. It simply means that such cannot be the main fare of the pulpit message. It means that, when uncertain, anxiety-producing issues must be plumbed, their burden should fall on, or be addressed to, a congregation prepared to grapple with them, probably in open dialogue.

Preaching or proclamation is the functional arm of dogmatic theology. "Dogmatic" is here used, in the best sense of the word, to mean the certain presentation of today's truth in its proper setting inside the historical message and meaning of Christianity. This is not to be construed as a reference to the stereotyped, hysterical, pulpit-pounding opposition of some preaching to science, reason, and modern thought in general. Of this Gerhard Ebeling says:

Yet it fails to realize its true obligation of presenting this man [a modern secular intellectual], whom it regards as the enemy whom it is incapable of loving, with the testimony which would bring him the gift of certainty. Church proclamation of this sort is *de facto* propaganda against the church. . . . What is really needed is that we should find a way of witnessing to the Christian faith which is so convincingly simple and radical as to overcome problems raised by the tension between the letter and the spirit, or at least to show that they are secondary problems.[1]

The Black hermeneutic, Black preaching at its best, has done this very thing time and again. Giving the primary emphasis to the immediate needs of people and putting the intellectual questions in their secondary place, the message for now has been proclaimed. An excellent illustration is found in a sermon preached by Sandy F. Ray many years ago at Bishop College:

This spirit to move out into new areas grips a man here and there. Not all, but one once in a while. Remember that thrilling story of the disciples caught in the storm. It involved a man of whom I am extremely fond. Jesus appeared and saw them out in the boat, distressed. The waters were lashing, and it was terribly dark. And they wished they had waited on him (because they had left him behind). And someone raised the question "I wonder where he is; we should never have left him!" "But he told us to go and he would be on later." "But now we are caught! We are caught in the grip of a storm and we can't manage this little boat."

And Jesus came, and the lightning flashed and somebody saw him, and when they saw him, they screamed, "Ghost! It's a ghost! It means that we are going to be destroyed!" And then the lightning flashed again, and Simon Peter saw him, and they all thought, "It's a ghost."

But just in the height of the fear, Jesus said, "Stop being afraid . . . it is I." And this daring man, with reckless faith, said, "Lord, if it be thou, suffer me to come to you walking on the water." He said, "Come on." So Simon started to leave the boat, and the other men laid a restraining hand on him and said, "Don't be stupid. . . . Be practical! . . . You've been about lakes all of your life. Haven't you had enough?" But he said, "Jesus told me to come." But they said, "Listen, we all love him, and we all know he has great power, but that's *water*, Simon, and no man has ever walked on water!" But Peter said, "That's the Lord." They said, "We know it's the Lord, but be practical!" But Simon said, "When the Lord calls, sometimes you lose the sense of what is practical, and right now my faith has become reckless and daring, and I'm going." And the records said, "He walked on the water!"

Oh, I know, I know you're going to say, "But he sank." . . . But he walked . . . he walked on the water! And when he started from the boat, the laws of nature said, "Here comes a man walking, Lord, on the water; and you know that this is against the laws of gravitation; what shall I do?" He said, "With faith like this, you might suspend the natural laws, because we have to meet a faith like this with an unusual suspension of the law. And if he has the faith to walk . . . let him walk!" And the records said, "He walked on the water." Oh, I know you said he sank. . . . But he walked! He walked long enough for it to go in his obituary that he walked on the water. But he was walking toward someone who could rescue him when he sank.

Let us make man . . . make him daring . . . make him venturesome . . . make him fearless . . . for he isn't completed yet and his task is not completed. There is lots yet to be done that calls for courage and strength and a daring and reckless faith. We won't all get it . . . but we can create a climate in which one man will walk on the water. We won't all try something great . . . but we can create a climate of faith in God that once in a while a prophet can grow up. Let us make man . . . he isn't finished yet.[2]

Thus did a Black preacher inspire a host of Black college students to attempt the theretofore impossible. Thus did he, in typical Black idiom, select his text on the basis of its message and not its scientific complexities. A certain sound was uttered about a certain issue, and the secondary matters were relegated to their rightful place.

The Message of Hope

This sermon by Sandy F. Ray also raises the issue of hope, so essential to the gospel as it must be preached to oppressed people. All humanity needs hope, but none so much as those who have so little other than hope. As the areas in which Black people can take up cudgels for themselves expand, their desperate need for hope may appear to diminish. But they will not soon be in the position to be numerically and physically in control, or even guaranteed justice, save by the hope that is in their faith. The most effective blows for freedom will still come from persons who, like Martin Luther King, Jr., believe in so hopeful a concept as "cosmic companionship" (preached to foot-weary walkers in Montgomery) that they just keep working. Their gospel of God's "somehow" told our ancestors that slavery would end. It told marchers that segregation would die, and it is still telling Blacks in South Africa that the day of justice is inevitable.

The sermons of Martin Luther King, Jr., are an excellent example of Black preaching as help from God. They share in the goals of God. The Presbyterian Shorter Catechism holds that the chief end of humanity is to glorify God and to enjoy God forever. Black preaching does not deny this. It simply holds that no sermon glorifies God which avoids God's plan to uplift humanity. Far from a secular, humanistic requirement, this stems from the admonition that, when the hearers perceive and receive the help of the gospel, they will in fact glorify God who is in heaven (Matt. 5:16).

Black preaching of the Reconstruction Era could be considered a tremendous success when it simply enabled Blacks to survive massive brutality and injustice. The church-aided organization of Black insurance companies and other businesses was virtually a stroke of genius. E. Franklin Frazier's *The Negro Church in America* describes the church's role in this crucial, Black-power-type thrust.[3] Black preachers more than any other single group were able to mobilize the saints who marched and marched in the sixties, until the walls came tumbling down. But the Black pulpit simply cannot coast on its golden ages. It must give Blacks the insights and inspiration to survive in today's social jungle, while, at the same time, arming them with the insights and inspiration to liberate themselves and eliminate oppression.

For instance, the Black preacher must keep the vivid imagery of the eagle stirring her nest (Deut. 32:11), a text dearly loved in the Black church. But, faced with the growing-up problems in the ghetto family, the preacher must emphasize the awesome wisdom of the eagle, who knows when to insist that the eaglet fly on its own. One uses the old images, but one gives a certain sound concerning young adults, so that Black parents will not be threatened by the loss of the one being in regard to whom they have exercised any real power. Parents will indeed glorify God in response, for they will see their problems as they have never seen them in secular terms. Youth, too, will be grateful for the easing of the rites of passage by seeing themselves in a new relation to the eagle's nest.

Along with this very personal kind of preaching help, the Black preacher must also give the certain sound that helps by mobilizing the Black church as the largest and most stable of all Black power bases. As a preacher summons the Black sisters to boycotts, which they more than anyone else can make effective, the clear implications of the book of Esther must be heard. They are indeed in the kingdom for such a time as this. And if they are scorned or even roughed up, what is this when compared with Esther, who said, "If I perish, I perish" (Esther 4:14-16)?

Texts like these are familiar and pregnant with the great joy that comes from fresh renditions and applications. These texts also have great potential for the help and empowerment of the congregation right here and now. Emotional reinforcement is given to the point of practical commitment by means of the tremendous fulfillment that comes from the hearers' identification with the heroines and heroes and their triumphs under God.

The Importance of Celebration

The sermon that celebrates without giving help is an opiate. The sermon that tries to help without celebration is, at least in the Black church, ineffective. The celebration is a necessity. But this is not to canonize a quaint cultural habit. Rather, it is to theologize concerning this important aspect of Black preaching, an element needed, in fact, in all preaching.

Highly liturgical churches refer to their priests as "celebrating" the mass. (The actual history of this term would be interesting indeed.) It is not necessary to legitimate joy and celebration in worship. The fruit of the spirit is joy (Gal. 5:22). The baby of Pentecostal joy must not be thrown out with what some may consider the bath water of public glossolalia or speaking in tongues. In modern times, the joy of Black worship has been self-validating to all save the most closed-minded. The "high" sought by the drug culture has been recognized by more than one ex-addict as inferior to the joy of Black worship.

What is the theological soundness of this mass expression? To say that Black worship succeeds in evoking joy is not to say that it is necessarily valid. Just as the joy of the spiritus sanctus (Holy Spirit) was confused with the joy of spiritus frumenti (alcohol) in the eyes of the unbelieving (Acts 2), so is it possible to confuse spirits in the church today.

At its best, however, Black worship must have joy in its highest and purest form. At their best, Black preachers must not only be teachers and mobilizers, parent figures and enablers, but they also must be celebrants. They must have a little of the joy themselves. It must be clear that they are filled with the same joy they declare to their congregations. If, indeed, preachers have not tasted and seen that it is good, they have nothing, really, to say. The goodness of God must not be a distant theory; it must be a present fact, which to experience is to celebrate. The same can be said of the goodness of the life that God gives.

To sense the presence and complete acceptance of God, especially when one lives in an unaccepting, hostile world, is to know joy unspeakable. If this is literally true, then how may one hold one's peace? Even if one has Western-oriented cultural inhibitions, given an open mind, one cannot fail to take part vicariously in the joy of the fellow celebrants, be they laity or clergy. In their pilgrimage through the torture chamber of three hundred and fifty years of oppression, this celebration of the goodness of God and his acceptance of persons has been the strongest nourishment available to Black people. It has reinforced and celebrated identity scorned everywhere else.

Of course, the Black church itself has been made to think of its freedom of expression as a sign of primitiveness. Witness the fact that Blacks sober up and get "dignified" in most churches when they have White visitors. This is now on the wane, and fortunately, this kind of covert self-rejection has never prevailed sufficiently to destroy the catharsis and healing of the shouting, celebrating Black church. If Blacks, who have had the best reasons for self-destruction, have left suicide statistically to White males, then the Black preacher mustn't stop celebrating now! And those who do not know how to celebrate should learn the art. In Black-worship celebration, selfhood is validated, identity is reinforced, and the courage-to-be is renewed in the accepting, healing, uplifting presence of God. Since little else in the world can accomplish this for Blacks, there seems to be not only theological validity but also practical validity for holding on to so vital a tradition.

*   *   *

To assert so much about the Black preacher's role in a day of diminishing faith is to suggest a Black tradition about the call of the minister which is no longer widely shared in the typical White church. Middle-class religion may prefer the conversational tone in preaching, also insisting that the preacher blend into the socioeconomic and political patterns of the laity. Black preachers know better. If Jeremiah could be called before birth (Jer. 1:5), so can they. And if Jeremiah's call could sustain him through unbelievable trials and rebuffs, a call from God can do the same for Black preachers. And it has. In a day when the Black preacher has to play many roles and be a multitude of things to all persons, especially to Blacks, it would be easier to escape the call for a less taxing responsibility were it not for the "fire shut up in my bones" (Jer. 20:9). The priesthood of all believers is a fact, but the burden of the priesthood still falls heavily on the Black preacher. Today's educated young Blacks would probably avoid the call in larger numbers were it not for the fact that the verse "woe is unto me, if I preach not the gospel!" (I Cor. 9:16) is still a powerful stimulus in the Black tradition.

These are some of the theological assumptions that underlie Black preaching. To engage in the business of Black preaching without such undergirding is either to be wanting in sincerity or to labor without support. In either case, it is to attempt the impossible, and to fail. Black preachers cannot afford merely to seem Black. If they have not the Black theological frame of reference, then they ought to preach from the frame of reference that they do have, and where it fits. Meanwhile, this distinctive tradition will offer much to all traditions and will receive much from those traditions in return, until in the providence of God we become one.

Notes

1. Why *Black* Preaching?

1. Alan Geyer, "Toward a Convivial Theology," *The Christian Century*, vol. 86, no. 17 (April 23, 1969), p. 542.
2. Gerhard Ebeling, *Word and Faith*, trans. James W. Teitch (Philadelphia: Fortress Press, 1963), pp. 9, 11.
3. John Dillenberger, "On Broadening the New Hermeneutic," *The New Hermeneutic*, James M. Robinson and John B. Cobb, Jr., eds. (New York: Harper & Row, 1964), vol. 2, p. 162.
4. A new book, by Stephen Reid, *Experience and Tradition: A Primer in Black Biblical Hermeneutics*, is forthcoming in 1991 from Abingdon Press.
5. Lerone Bennett, Jr., *The Negro Mood* (Chicago: Johnson Publishing Co., 1964), p. 73.

2. A History of Black Preaching

1. David Henry Bradley, Sr., *A History of the A.M.E. Zion Church* (Nashville: Parthenon Press, 1956), p. 29.
2. Leslie H. Fishel, Jr., and Benjamin Quarles, *The Negro American: A Documentary History* (Glenview, Ill.: Scott, Foresman, and Co., 1967), pp. 36-37.
3. Carter G. Woodson, *The History of the Negro Church* (Washington, D.C.: Associated Publishers, 1921), pp. 7-9.
4. David Walker, *An Appeal* (New York: Arno Press and The New York Times, 1829, 1969), pp. 27, 38, 39.
5. Woodson, *Negro Church*, pp. 17-20.
6. Henry H. Mitchell, *Black Belief* (New York: Harper & Row, 1975), pp. 99-101.
7. W. E. B. DuBois, *The Gift of Black Folk* (New York: Johnson Reprint Corp., 1924, 1968), p. 332.
8. Holland M. McTyeire, *A History of Methodism* (Nashville: Southern Methodist Publishing House, 1887), pp. 346-47.

9. Daniel A. Payne, *History of the African Methodist Episcopal Church* (Nashville: Publishing House of the A.M.E. Sunday School Union, 1891; reprint, New York: Johnson Reprint Corp., 1968), pp. 73-78.
10. Woodson, *Negro Church*, pp. 61-65.
11. DuBois, *Gift of Black*, p. 332.
12. Among the records is an excerpt from his journal reproduced in Fishel and Quarles, *Negro American*, pp. 70-72.
13. Edgar G. Thomas, *The First African Baptist Church of North America* (Savannah, Ga., 1925), p. 74.
14. The membership figures for the Savannah church show 381 in 1794, 800 in 1802, 1,712 in 1818, and 2,357 in 1829. Thomas, *First African Baptist*, pp. 39, 45, 47.
15. Thomas, *First African Baptist*, pp. 14-30.
16. Sidney E. Ahlstrom, *The Religious History of the American People* (Garden City, N.Y.: Doubleday and Co., 1975), vol. 1, p. 393.
17. Fishel and Quarles, *Negro American*, pp. 135-36.
18. Moses Grandy, "Narrative of the Life of Moses Grandy," in *Five Slave Narratives*, William Loren Katz, ed. (New York: Arno Press and The New York Times, 1969), pp. 35-36.
19. Frances Trollope, *Domestic Manners of the Americans*, quoted in Miles Mark Fisher, *Negro Slave Songs in the United States* (Ithaca, N.Y.: Cornell University Press, 1953; reprint, New York: Russell and Russell, 1968), p. 33.
20. DuBois, *Gift of Black*, p. 5.
21. Woodson, *Negro Church*, p. 305.
22. William H. Pipes, *Say Amen, Brother* (Westport, Conn.: Negro Universities Press, 1951, 1970), p. 60.
23. Benjamin Franklin, *Autobiography* (New York: Henry Holt and Co., 1916), pp. 196-98.
24. Vernon Loggins, *The Negro Author* (Port Washington, N.Y.: Kennikat Press, 1931), p. 4.
25. "The Life of Gustavus Vassa, the African" in Arna Bontemps, ed., *Great Slave Narratives* (Boston: Beacon Press, 1969), p. 99.
26. Ahlstrom, *Religious History*, p. 392.
27. George P. Rawick, *The American Slave: A Composite Autobiography* (Westport, Conn.: Greenwood Press, 1972), vol. 3, part 4, pp. 178-79.
28. J. V. Watson, *Tales and Takings, Sketches and Incidents, from the Itinerant and Editorial Budget of Rev. J. V. Watson, Editor of the Northwestern Christian Advocate* (New York: 1856), p. 87. Quoted in H. Dean Trulear and Russell Ritchey, "Two Sermons by Brother Carper: The Eloquent Negro Preacher," *American Baptist Quarterly*, vol. 6, no. 1 (March 1987), pp. 3-10.

3. Training for Black Preachers Through the Years

1. Daniel A. Payne, *History of the African Methodist Episcopal Church*, vol. 1 (Nashville: Publishing House of the A.M.E. Sunday School Union, 1891; reprint, New York: Johnson Reprint Corp., 1968), p. 89.
2. George F. Bragg, *History of the Afro-American Group of the Episcopal Church* (Baltimore: Church Advocate Press, 1922; reprint, New York: Johnson Reprint Corp., 1968), p. 76.
3. Daniel Coker, "A Dialogue Between a Virginian and an African Minister," in *Negro Protest Pamphlets*, Dorothy Porter, ed. (New York: Arno Press and The New York Times, 1969), p. 15.
4. Payne, *African Methodist*, p. 419.
5. Ibid., p. 16.

6. James W. Hood, *One Hundred Years of the African Methodist Episcopal Zion Church* (New York: A.M.E. Zion Book Concern, 1895), p. 166.
7. Payne, *African Methodist*, p. 277.
8. Ibid., p. vii.
9. Ibid., p. 235.
10. Charles S. Smith, *The History of the A.M.E. Church*, vol. 2 (Philadelphia: Book Concern of the A.M.E. Church, 1922; reprint, New York: Johnson Reprint Corp., 1968), pp. 126-27.
11. W. E. B. DuBois, *The Gift of Black Folk* (Boston: Stratford Co., 1924; reprint, New York: Johnson Reprint Corp., 1968), pp. 284-85.
12. Carter G. Woodson, *The History of the Negro Church* (Washington, D.C.: Associated Publishers, 1921), pp. 244-45.
13. W. E. B. DuBois, *The Souls of Black Folk* (Chicago: A. C. McClurg & Co., 1903; reprint, New York: Fawcett World Library, 1961), p. 84.
14. Payne, *African Methodist*, p. 419.
15. Smith, *A.M.E.*, pp. 191-92.
16. Edgar G. Thomas, *The First African Baptist Church of North America* (Savannah, Ga., 1925), p. 78.
17. Ibid., p. 83.
18. Ibid., p. 91.
19. Absalom Jones and Richard Allen, "A Narrative of the Proceedings of the Black People, During the Late Awful Calamity in Philadelphia, in the Year 1793," in *Negro Protest Pamphlets*, Dorothy Porter, ed. (New York: Arno Press and The New York Times, 1969).
20. Woodson, *Negro Church*, pp. 167-84.
21. Ernest J. Miller, "The Anti-Slavery Role of Henry Highland Garnet," (Unpublished S.T.M. Thesis, Union Theological Seminary, New York, N.Y., 1969).
22. Henry Highland Garnet, *An Address to the Slaves of the United States of America*, William L. Katz, ed. (New York: Arno Press and The New York Times, 1969), p. 93.
23. John Hope Franklin, *From Slavery to Freedom* (New York: Alfred A. Knopf, 1967), pp. 319-20.
24. William J. Simmons, *Men of Mark* (Geo. M. Rewell & Co., 1887; reprint, Chicago: Johnson Publishing Corp., 1970), pp. 613-14.
25. Lester F. Russell, *Black Baptist Secondary Schools in Virginia, 1887–1957* (Metuchen, N.J.: Scarecrow Press, 1981), pp. 50-51.
26. Woodson, *Negro Church*, pp. 224-25.
27. Simmons, *Men of Mark*, pp. 259-61.
28. Horace Mann Bond, *Education for Freedom* (Princeton, N.J.: Princeton University Press, 1976), pp. 442, 527.
29. Simmons, *Men of Mark*, pp. 70-74.
30. Charles E. Boddie, *Giant in the Earth* (Berne, Ind.: Berne Witness Co., 1945).
31. Miles Mark Fisher, *The Master's Slave, Elijah John Fisher* (Philadelphia: Judson Press, 1922).
32. Taylor Branch, *Parting the Waters* (New York: Simon & Schuster, 1988), pp. 8-9.

4. The Black Approach to the Bible

1. Henry H. Mitchell, *Black Belief* (New York: Harper & Row, 1975), pp. 12-30.
2. Howard Thurman, *Jesus and the Disinherited* (Nashville/New York: Abingdon-Cokesbury Press, 1949), pp. 30-31.

3. Benjamin E. Mays, *Born to Rebel: An Autobiography* (New York: Charles Scribner's Sons, 1971), p. 36.
4. Maya Angelou, *I Know Why the Caged Bird Sings* (New York: Random House, 1969), pp. 18, 26, 31, 55-56, 96-100, 191.
5. Richard E. Day, *Rhapsody in Black* (Valley Forge, Pa.: Judson Press, 1953), pp. 101-2.
6. Richard M. Dorson, *American Negro Folktales* (New York: Fawcett, 1967), p. 49.
7. Sandy F. Ray, unpublished address at the Baptist Congress of Christian Education (San Francisco, Calif., June 24, 1976).
8. Clarence Jordan, "The Rich Man and Lazarus, and Other Parables Retold for Our Time," a sound recording released by Koinonia Records, Tiskilwa, IL 61368.
9. Bill Moyers, "Foreword," in Samuel D. Proctor, *Samuel Proctor: My Moral Odyssey* (Valley Forge, Pa.: Judson Press, 1989), p. 11.

5. Preaching and the Mother Tongue of the Spirit

1. William Labov, *The Social Stratification of English in New York City* (Washington, D.C.: Center for Applied Linguistics, 1966), p. 482.

6. Personal Style in Black Preaching

1. Miles Mark Fisher, *Negro Slave Songs in the United States* (Ithaca, N.Y.: Cornell University Press, 1953; reprint, New York: Russell and Russell, 1968), pp. 1-13.
2. Ibid., p. 17.
3. A "Blackese" word meaning sedate.
4. S. M. Lockridge is pastor of Calvary Baptist Church, San Diego, Calif.

7. The Black Context for Preaching

1. Transcribed from an undated recording tape of Vernon Johns at the Hampton University Ministers' Conference. This was published in the first edition of *Black Preaching* (Philadelphia: J. B. Lippincott, 1970), p. 99; and in *Human Possibilities: A Vernon Johns Reader*, ed. Samuel L. Gandy (Washington, D.C.: Hoffman Press, 1977), p. 134.
2. Vernon Johns, the Hampton University Ministers' Conference, in *Black Preaching*, p. 106.
3. Sandy F. Ray, address at the Baptist Congress of Christian Education, San Francisco, Calif., June 24, 1976.

8. The Black Sermon

1. James Earl Massey, *Designing the Sermon* (Nashville: Abingdon, 1980), pp. 21-22.
2. Ibid., p. 23.
3. Fred B. Craddock, *Overhearing the Gospel* (Nashville: Abingdon, 1978).
4. See Henry Mitchell's book, *Celebration and Experience in Preaching* (Abingdon Press, 1990) for an extensive discussion of holistic preaching.
5. Sandy F. Ray, late minister of the Cornerstone Baptist Church of Brooklyn, N.Y., and vice-president of the National Baptist Convention, U.S.A., Inc. This sermon was preached at several funerals.

9. Toward a Theology of Black Preaching

1. Gerhard Ebeling, *Theology and Proclamation*, trans. R. Gregor Smith (Philadelphia: Fortress Press, 1966), p. 19.

2. Sandy F. Ray, from a sermon at Bishop College, Dallas, Texas.

3. E. Franklin Frazier, *The Negro Church in America* (New York: Schocken Books, 1963), pp. 34-38.

Bibliography

Ahlstrom, Sidney E. *The Religious History of the American People*, 2 vols. Garden City, N.Y.: Doubleday and Co., 1975.

Angelou, Maya. *I Know Why the Caged Bird Sings*. New York: Random House, 1969.

Bennet, Lerone, Jr. *The Negro Mood*. Chicago: Johnson Publishing Co., 1964.

Boddie, Charles E. *Giant in the Earth*. Berne, Ind.: Berne Witness Co., 1965.

———. *God's "Bad Boys."* Valley Forge, Pa.: Judson Press, 1972.

Bond, Horace Mann. *Education for Freedom*. Princeton, N.J.: Princeton University Press, 1976.

Bradley, David Henry, Sr. *A History of the A.M.E. Zion Church*. Nashville: Parthenon Press, 1956.

Bragg, George F. *History of the Afro-American Group of the Episcopal Church*. Baltimore: Church Advocate Press, 1922; reprint, New York: Johnson Reprint Corp., 1968.

Branch, Taylor. *Parting the Waters*. New York: Simon & Schuster, 1988.

Coker, Daniel. "A Dialogue Between a Virginian and an African Minister." *Negro Protest Pamphlets*, Dorothy Porter, ed. New York: Arno Press and The New York Times, 1969.

Craddock, Fred B. *Overhearing the Gospel*. Nashville: Abingdon Press, 1978.

Day, Richard E. *Rhapsody in Black*. Valley Forge, Pa.: Judson Press, 1953.

Dillenberger, John. "On Broadening the New Hermeneutic." *The New Hermeneutic*. James M. Robinson and John B. Cobb, Jr., eds. New York: Harper & Row, 1964.

DuBois, W. E. B. *The Gift of Black Folk*. Boston: Stratford Co., 1924; reprint, New York: Johnson Reprint Corp., 1968.
_____. *The Souls of Black Folk*. Chicago: A. C. McClurg & Co., 1903; New York: Fawcett World Library, 1961.

Ebeling, Gerhard. *Theology and Proclamation*, trans. R. Gregor Smith. Philadelphia: Fortress Press, 1966.
_____. *Word and Faith*, trans. James W. Teitch. Philadelphia: Fortress Press, 1963.

Fishel, Leslie H., Jr., and Benjamin Quarles. *The Negro American: A Documentary History*. Glenview, Ill.: Scott, Foresman, and Co., 1967.
Fisher, Miles Mark. *Negro Slave Songs in the United States*. Ithaca, N.Y.: Cornell University Press, 1953; reprint, New York: Russell and Russell, 1968.
_____. *The Master's Slave, Elijah John Fisher*. Philadelphia: Judson Press, 1922.
Franklin, John Hope. *From Slavery to Freedom*. New York: Alfred A. Knopf, 1967.
Frazier, E. Franklin. *The Negro Church in America*. New York: Schocken Books, 1963.

Geyer, Alan. "Toward A Convivial Theology." *The Christian Century*. Vol. 86, no. 17, April 23, 1969.
Grandy, Moses. "Narrative of the Life of Moses Grandy." *Five Slave Narratives*, William Loren Katz, ed. New York: Arno Press and The New York Times, 1969.

Hood, James W. *One Hundred Years of the African Methodist Episcopal Zion Church*. New York: A.M.E. Zion Book Concern, 1895.

Jones, Absalom, and Richard Allen. "A Narrative of the Proceedings of the Black People, During the Late Awful Calamity in Philadelphia, in the Year 1793." *Negro Protest Pamphlets*, Dorothy Porter, ed. New York: Arno Press and The New York Times, 1969.
Jordan, Clarence. "The Rich Man and Lazarus, and Other Parables Retold for Our Time," a sound recording. Tiskilwa, Ill.: Koinonia Records.

Labov, William. *The Social Stratification of English in New York City*. Washington, D.C.: Center for Applied Linguistics, 1966.
Loggins, Vernon. *The Negro Author*. Port Washington, N.Y.: Kennikat Press, 1931.

McTyeire, Holland M. *A History of Methodism*. Nashville: Southern Methodist Publishing House, 1887.
Massey, James Earl. *Designing the Sermon*. Nashville: Abingdon, 1980.
Mays, Benjamin E. *Born to Rebel: An Autobiography*. New York: Charles Scribner's Sons, 1971.

Miller, Ernest J. "The Anti-slavery Role of Henry Highland Garnet." Unpublished S.T.M. Thesis, Union Theological Seminary, New York, N.Y., 1969.

Mitchell, Henry H. *Black Belief.* New York: Harper & Row, 1975.

Moyers, Bill. "Foreword." In Samuel D. Proctor, *Samuel Proctor: My Moral Odyssey.* Valley Forge, Pa.: Judson Press, 1989.

Payne, Daniel A. *History of the African Methodist Episcopal Church.* Nashville: Publishing House of the A.M.E. Sunday School Union, 1891; reprint, New York: Johnson Reprint Corp., 1968.

Pipes, William H. *Say Amen, Brother.* New York: William-Frederick Press, 1951; reprint, Westport, Conn.: Negro Universities Press, 1970.

Rawick, George P. *The American Slave: A Composite Autobiography.* Westport, Conn.: Greenwood Press, 1972.

Russell, Lester F. *Black Baptist Secondary Schools in Virginia, 1887–1957.* Metuchen, N.J.: Scarecrow Press, 1981.

Simmons, William J. *Men of Mark.* Chicago: Johnson Publishing Co., 1970.

Smith, Charles S. *The History of the A.M.E. Church,* vol. 2. Philadelphia: Book Concern of the A.M.E. Church, 1922; reprint, New York: Johnson Reprint Corp., 1968.

Thomas, Edgar G. *The First African Baptist Church of North America.* Savannah, Ga., 1925.

Thurman, Howard. *Jesus and the Disinherited.* Nashville/New York: Abingdon-Cokesbury Press, 1949.

Trollope, Frances, *Domestic Manners of the Americans,* quoted in Miles Mark Fisher. *Negro Slave Songs in the United States.* Ithaca, N.Y.: Cornell University Press, 1953; reprint, New York: Russell and Russell, 1968.

Walker, David. *An Appeal.* New York: Arno Press and The New York Times, 1829, 1969.

Watson, J. V. *Tales and Takings, Sketches and Incidents, from the Itinerant and Editorial Budget of Rev. J. V. Watson, Editor of the Northwestern Christian Advocate.* New York: 1856. Quoted in H. Dean Trulear and Russell Ritchey. "Two Sermons by Brother Carper: The Eloquent Negro Preacher." *American Baptist Quarterly,* vol. 6, no. 1, March 1987.

Woodson, Carter G. *The History of the Negro Church.* Washington, D.C.: Associated Publishers, 1921.

Index